D0429312

THE PIE LIFE

A GUILT-FREE RECIPE FOR
SUCCESS AND SATISFACTION

SAMANTHA ETTUS

Published in Los Angeles, California, by Ghost Mountain Books, Inc.

ISBN:
Print 978-1-939457-23-3   **33614057724576**
EPub 978-1-939457-51-6
Mobi 978-1-939457-52-3

Cover Photo: Karey Roe
Cover Design: Longerday.com and Citrus Studios
Interior Design and Production: Dovetail Publishing Services

For my treasured trio: Ella, Ruby, and Bowen.

May you always lead a life you love.

CONTENTS

Note to Readers

This book is comprised of the opinions and ideas of its author, who is neither a medical, health, psychology, nor a psychiatric professional. The contents of this book is meant solely for general informational and entertainment purposes on the subjects addressed in the book. The author and publisher are not engaged in the rendering of medical, health, psychological, or psychiatric professional services within this book. The ideas and concepts in this book are not intended to diagnose, treat, cure, or prevent any medical, health, mental, physical, psychological or psychiatric problem or condition, nor are they meant to substitute for professional advice of any kind. The reader should consult his or her medical, health, psychological, or other competent professional before adopting any of the concepts in this book or drawing inferences from it. The content of this book, by its very nature, is general, whereas each reader's situation is unique. Therefore, as with all books of this nature, the purpose is to provide general information rather than address individual situations, which books by their very nature cannot do.

The author and publisher specifically disclaim all responsibility for, and are not liable for, any liability, loss, or risk, personal or otherwise, which is incurred as a consequence, directly or indirectly, of the use and application of any of the contents of this book.

Any and all product names referenced within this book are copyright and trademarks of their respective owners. None of these owners have sponsored, authorized, endorsed, or approved this book in any way. Unless otherwise noted, the author is in no way affiliated with any brands or products recommended in this book.

INTRODUCTION

My then five-year-old daughter Ella sat in the kitchen eating breakfast and talking excitedly about her upcoming school play. She looked up as she heard me gasp. "What's wrong, Mommy?"

"Oh, nothing, love."

How I wished that were true. Ella's first kindergarten performance was scheduled for the same day as a critical business event I had committed to six months earlier. While she would be singing her heart out on stage in Los Angeles, I would be in Boston speaking to 8,000 women gathered at the Massachusetts Conference for Women. I felt overcome with guilt; my daughter would be devastated to hear I wouldn't be there for her big performance. And I desperately wanted to attend. Of the many shapes and sizes of mommy guilt, this was Mount Everest.

This didn't mean I was prepared to miss my speech; it just meant that I needed to think of a backup plan—and fast. I contacted my mom friend who travels the most and she suggested the dress rehearsal. Of course! Why hadn't I thought of that?! I would attend the dress rehearsal and my husband would also video her part for me at the main event. With this plan in place, I delivered the news and Ella was surprisingly satisfied. Another messy moment had bitten the dust.

I've coached thousands of women over the years—working moms, single moms, stay-at-home moms, on-ramping moms, stepmoms, C-level moms. I've spoken to thousands more who've called in to my radio show. They have all experienced moments like this, times when they felt they just couldn't keep up. Sadly, many have reacted by changing or giving up on their careers because of these messy moments. Blaming their job for their imperfect personal life, they've cut back their hours, looked for a more "family friendly" career, or left the workforce entirely. The thing is that stay-at-home moms have all had these moments too, but as working moms, we rush to blame our careers. When I asked journalist Lisa Belkin for her thoughts on this topic, having covered it in her now famous 2003 "Opt-Out Revolution" piece for the *New York Times,* she said, "We go into jobs for rational reasons and leave them for emotional ones." I have seen this time and again—women making snap decisions at challenging moments rather than taking a step back, letting things settle, and considering the big picture before acting.

Don't Even *Think* About It

Before we go any further, let's take that option off the table. If you feel squeezed between work and family responsibilities, please know that the *worst* thing you could do is give up your career. Research shows that the happiest among us, the ones who enjoy their lives most and feel fulfilled, are those with thriving personal lives *and* successful careers. This doesn't mean that our personal and professional lives won't conflict, or that we won't feel the pain of having to make constant sacrifices. Of course we will. It just means that the effort is well worth it.

When pharmaceutical executive and mom of three, Lauren Wilson returned to work after the birth of her youngest child, she found herself driving home on the freeway, pumping breast milk, and on a conference call, muted so no one would hear the pump. This hazardous multitasking could have pushed her over the edge, but instead, on tough days like this one, Lauren reminds herself that "by working, I have decision power."

Some women reason that they don't have to work because they feel their spouses make "enough" money. They forget that the baby years are short and our lives are long. The sad statistical reality is that more than 70 percent of women who return to work after taking only two years off can't find a position comparable to what they had before.[1] Their happiness plummets along with their paychecks. We women like to use our whole selves—our bodies, our minds, our energy. When we don't, we feel less fulfilled.

I attended a barbecue last summer hosted by a couple with a healthy six-month-old baby. The dad, a finance executive, talked about how hard it was for his attorney wife to decide whether to remain at her job. His wife worked from nine to six and then made it home to put their son to bed each night. On Fridays she worked from home. It sounded to me like she had won the working mom jackpot. Yet her husband was still grappling with whether she (not he!) should continue to work. Finally I turned to him. "What would it feel like for *you*," I said, "if beginning tomorrow, your entire life centered around Jack's sleep and feeding schedule—if you just focused on him all day long?"

Stunned, he admitted he had never thought about it that way. Unprompted, he then launched into a description of his wife's background. He proudly described how she had been class president in high school, on the dean's list in college, and a starter on the field hockey team. Then she had gone to law school, where she edited the law review. "You're right," he said. "There's no way she could give all this up any more than I could, no matter how much we love our son." As he subsequently told me, his conversations with his wife from that point on were never the same.

The Bigger Picture

Susan Riles was a neighbor in our apartment building whom I had known since early childhood. One day when I was 11, my mom turned to me and said, "Mrs. Riles can't stand her husband, but she is stuck in that marriage forever because she has no money of her own." It was the first time I was introduced to the relationship between income and power. I remember my shock and the overwhelming wave of empathy I felt for Mrs. Riles.

It isn't just about our own well-being. My husband always said that our whole family would suffer if I stayed home because I would put all of my unused energy into our kids and that would just make them anxious. New studies show that he was on to something. Helicopter parenting stifles children's natural progression toward independence, making them worried and stressed. It can also make them poorer. Research shows that the sons of working moms help out more in the home as adults, and the daughters of working moms earn more when they get jobs of their own. A recent study shows that daughters of working moms in the United States earn *23 percent* more than daughters of stay-at-home moms.[2]

Beyond your family and your own well-being, I believe you owe it to *humanity* to work. The comedian and mom Tina Fey understands how a woman's decision to work or stay home can impact the wider world. In her best-selling book *Bossypants,* she writes that almost 200 people worked on her television show with her. "If I flaked out and quit, their jobs would disappear," she recognizes. Fey honors this sense of responsibility—and delivers on it. While you might not have 200 employees working on your product or business like Fey, the concept is true for you too. Anything you can share and contribute beyond your four walls benefits the larger world.

We talk so much about giving back to our communities, but what better way to make a difference than to touch the greatest number of people with your gifts? If you're a talented artist who stops working to focus on your family, you are depriving the world of your creations. If you're a corporate lawyer who quits your job, the women in your firm lose you as a mentor and your clients lose out on great ideas. Imagine how the world would be impacted if New York Senator Kirsten Gillibrand had decided to stay home instead of running for office, or if Colorado-based Sergeant Edna Hendershot had opted out and not put one of the biggest serial rapists in history behind bars,[3] or how many young girls would not have found their idol if Olympian Kerri Walsh Jennings had quit while pregnant with her third child instead of continuing to train and win her third gold medal. These examples are extreme, but each and every woman in the workforce becomes a role model for the women following their trail, and they often are the ones to carry the women up through the ranks. If the experienced women disappear from the workforce, who is left to help the young women behind them?

The Question

Once you recognize that "to work or not to work" is a question that may set you up for lack of fulfillment and other problems down the road, the question should become how to organize and manage your life to make it as full, rich, and fulfilling as possible. So many women in the workplace are just "surviving," trying to get through the day. If this sounds like you—frazzled, sleep deprived, overwhelmed, and unhappy—then it's time to start loving your life, not just living it.

Most of us haven't figured out how best to manage lives that contain multiple parts to them. We embrace all sorts of conventional metaphors and lingo to convey what we're trying to accomplish as women who work—"balancing" our different roles, "juggling" our responsibilities, doing our best to "have it all." In the absence of a better set of ideas that will help us both in normal times and moments of crisis, these media-fed descriptions have been filling our heads, subtly encouraging us to blame ourselves. We can never match up to the ideal of perfection implied by having it all, and as a result we inevitably feel guilty and stuck. We wind up "settling" by reconciling ourselves to jobs, spouses, friends, or living situations we don't really enjoy. We don't thrive; we survive. We live each day just trying to keep our head above water.

That's not good enough. We need something different. This book gives it to you. It will change your life, as well as those of your family, colleagues, friends, and neighbors.

Your Life . . . As a Pie

I've always seen life a bit differently given my untraditional childhood. As a young girl growing up in New York City, I was one of the top 100 female tennis players in the United States in my age group. Achieving and maintaining that ranking was my "job." I would leave school early each day, drive to tennis an hour away, play for two hours, drive another hour back, eat dinner at 7:00 p.m., and do my three hours of homework. Afterward, I spent a half hour on the phone talking to friends and went to sleep by 11:00 p.m. The next day, I started the routine all over again. I spent my weekends at tennis tournaments hours from my home.

With a teenage life like this, I was always contending with competing demands on my time, energy, and focus. Somehow, I had to figure out how to fit it all in and still make time for fun. I coped by thinking of my existence in separate categories. I'm not sure what made me do this—I just did it naturally. Lying in bed at night, I divided my life into various areas and evaluated how I was doing in each one. These categories included school (how were my grades?); family (had I fought with my mom?); tennis (what was my ranking?); boys (did he like me?); and friends (did my friendships feel solid?). The categories didn't all matter equally to me. Some were more important, and I tried to put special effort into those areas. To make it all work, I devised techniques, strategies, and tricks that would help me get the most out of each area, without neglecting any of them. I loved thinking about my life in terms of categories because it made my existence feel fuller and more whole—and when a category wasn't going well, I could keep it in its own compartment and work on improving it rather than letting it bleed into the other areas of my life.

Through college and into adulthood, I continued to monitor the categories of my life, and my techniques and strategies multiplied in turn. The labels shifted slightly over time, and the stakes felt higher and more out of my control, but the practice of dividing up the areas of my life persisted.

Today I continue to believe that life is best lived when you think of it as a pie, with you as the baker. Not just any pie. *Your* pie. The different "slices" correspond to the many areas of your life that you define as important.

There are six or seven basic categories that our lives fall into: career (which I hope you will now consider nonnegotiable), children (if you have them or plan to), health, relationship (or the quest to find one), community, friends, and hobbies. We all have multiple parts of our lives that we must honor in order to feel fulfilled, and at different stages of our life, certain slices become more important and others fade a bit. Today you might want love, sex, and good friends. You might want healthy, beautiful, happy children. You might want to make money and succeed professionally. In just a few years, your hobbies might hit the back burner as you make it through the more labor-intensive baby years. I have found that the best way to manage the many pieces is to conceive of them as a perfect whole, a complete circle with nothing missing. When all the slices of your pie are in place, you're left with a creation that is wholesome and satisfying—a rich, full, and complete existence. This is the life you were meant to live. It's the delicious and nurturing life you deserve.

As I've worked with women on their work/life management tactics, I've been struck by just how well the initial categories from my teen years match up with our adult lives. I've coached Fortune 500 CEOs, celebrities, Olympians, and groups of thousands of everyday women, from executive assistants to bloggers to the women who call my radio show every week. Again and again, the Pie Life philosophy has worked, in many cases changing women's lives. I've refined and perfected my approach over the years, adjusting it as social norms, work conditions, and women's lives have changed. But all along, the core concept of the Pie Life has remained the same.

Baking *Your* Pie

If you're yearning to get the very best out of your family life and your career and don't quite know how, the Pie Life is for you. The chapters that follow share dozens of secrets and strategies used by some of the world's most accomplished women to manage the seemingly impossible demands they face, and to even have fun doing it. But I won't just give you a new tip or two. My larger goal is to "disrupt" how you live and run your life. In business, we use the term "disruptive innovation" for something that shakes up an existing market and creates a new one. I want to disrupt your lifestyle so that you enjoy what I and other women I know have achieved—a lasting, sustainable makeover from the inside out. For that you need to start from scratch, turning upside down how you think about your life and grasping a new, completely accessible framework.

HOW DELICIOUS IS YOUR CURRENT PIE—REALLY?

1. To you, work/life balance means:
   A. "Don't look too closely, I haven't shaved my legs in a week!"
   B. "All work, no play makes Jane a dull girl."
   C. "I'm at the playground now and I miss working."

2. The last time you went on date night was:
   A. This week!
   B. Months ago.
   C. Date night? I remember those.

3. Finish this sentence. My sleep schedule . . .
   A. is as predictable as Big Ben.
   B. changes like the wind.
   C. I'll sleep when I'm dead.

4. My friends feel . . .
   A. that I will be there for them if they need me.
   B. surprised to see me but excited when they do.
   C. I am someone they never see anymore.

5. My career . . .
   A. is going great.
   B. needs a jump start.
   C. is an exciting past life I dimly remember.

6. My child's teacher . . .
   A. knows me well.
   B. understands how busy I am.
   C. wouldn't recognize me in a lineup.

Scoring: A = 5 points; B = 3 points; C = 1 point. If you scored between 24 and 30, your life looks delicious. Between 14 and 23, it needs more spice. Between 6 and 13, sorry, it's half baked.

The opening chapters of this book explore our quest for a richer, more exciting life as well as the traps that hold us back. I'll then introduce the concept of the Pie Life in more detail, helping you figure out what *you* want your pie to taste like (your vision for your life), what critical ingredients you'll need during the baking, and how you might best slice up your pie (what areas of life matter most to you). Then I'll go deeper into the key slices: career, children, health, relationship, community, friends, and hobbies. I'll share with you proven techniques and strategies that will help you make your life easier, so that you can accomplish more with less time and effort. I'll close the book by offering reflections on how best to enjoy the delicious pie you've baked for yourself.

The great thing about the Pie Life is that you are the baker. You choose the flavor, tweak the ingredients, and slice the pie to your specifications. You already have a fully baked pie—you just haven't discovered it yet. It's when you can see yourself as baker and take control of the final product that you will feel a sea change. Then life starts to feel more purposeful and energizing. Every day brings exciting new challenges and growth. You will no longer be surviving—you will be thriving, and accomplishing things you never thought possible.

Of course, life doesn't suddenly become perfect. It doesn't have to be; the yummiest pies are often the messy, gooey ones. When I was running my first company, I had to cancel a long-planned vacation to land a new client that would eventually put my firm on the map. More recently, when I missed out on my daughter Ella's school performance, I made peace with it by knowing I was impacting the lives of hundreds of women. And no, I didn't beat myself up endlessly. In that case, I made the alternative dress rehearsal plan and stuck to it. Pursuing wholeness in life often feels this way to me: countless sacrifices along the way, but with a payback that makes it all worth it.

The Pie Life will help you give your life the makeover of your dreams. No matter your age or means, this book contains the ultimate recipe for your most fulfilling lifestyle, complete with better relationships, more satisfying work, and more fun. You don't have to be perfect to adopt the Pie Life; I'm not waiting for you to drop 10 pounds or snag the big promotion or find your Prince Charming. You are wonderful as you are and you have everything you need *right now*. So let's mix up the ingredients in a brand new way.

Let's start living the Pie Life.

PART I

PREP

CHAPTER ONE

ALL THE SATISFACTION, NONE OF THE GUILT

The most difficult thing is the decision to act, the rest is merely tenacity.

— AMELIA EARHART

In late 2014, I stepped off the "Confidence Bus" at Newark, New Jersey's Prudential Center to participate in Oprah's "The Life You Want Weekend," a 48-hour dose of heavy-duty empowerment featuring Oprah and such top self-help figures as Deepak Chopra and Elizabeth Gilbert. The Confidence Bus was a place for attendees (a combination of hard-core Oprah fans and other women seeking inspiration and motivation) to gather some quick encouragement, makeup applications, hair styling—and advice from me.

The parking lot had been transformed into a vast pop-up theme park of hospitality tents designed to resemble a town square. Thousands of attendees filtered through the tents during breaks between segments on the main stage. I had been asked to give my signature "lifestyle makeovers," mini versions of the help I offer to callers on my radio program each week. In a one-hour show, I typically field four calls from a mix of working moms and dads asking for advice on problems ranging from the gargantuan (a fiancé who had relapsed back into a drug problem) to the more typical (an inability to figure out a career path, when to introduce a new boyfriend to a child, how to help an unmotivated teen, or how to get a spouse to pitch in more at home). While most experts offer reflective listening or minor suggestions, I like to offer solutions to the big stuff and recommend substantial change to get people to improve their lives that much faster. In other words, I recommend a complete makeover—kind of like the ambush makeovers you see on morning talk shows, where a frumpy woman is transformed into a beauty queen in minutes. The only difference: my makeovers are about the inside—how we are managing our lives and the internal changes we must make to live the best lives possible.

"I only cry when it rains."

Over 48 hours at Oprah's event, I gave lifestyle makeovers to 140 women from all walks of life—from nurses and real estate agents to teachers and social workers. Each attendee had two minutes to tell me her problem, and in two minutes I offered a response. It was like speed dating—for advice. Although our time was short, I heard these women, held their hands, and proposed solutions.

Dara, one of the first women I worked with, was a fiftyish, strong, and stylish woman with short hair. As Dara told me, she gives of herself to everyone—her mom, her kids, her husband. Recently, her well had run dry because she had lost her support system. Her sister-in-law, the one person in whom she confided regularly, had died suddenly of cancer. To make matters worse, Dara was laid off from her big job in city government and settled for a child-care job that she hated. She regrets that she never graduated from college, a reality that has also limited her job prospects. She now feels too fragile to take care of anyone. "They don't know how weak I really am. I only cry when it rains," she told me.

I was taken with Dara because she appeared strong and spoke without a hint of self-pity, yet inside she felt tormented, overwhelmed, disappointed with herself, and so trapped in her current reality that she couldn't even begin to conceive of how to change it.

Then I met Anna, a brunette in her late thirties. She worked six days a week managing a restaurant, her husband worked two shifts at a factory, and she had a 4-year-old daughter. Anna felt like she and her husband were at one another's throats and that she and her daughter didn't have enough time together. Like Dara, she felt stuck in her life and didn't know what she could do to free herself.

One week after the Oprah event, while sitting on 40th Street in the heart of midtown Manhattan, I encountered this paralysis and insecurity again among an entirely different demographic of women. It was Advertising Week, an annual conference for the top executives in marketing, and I was giving similar lifestyle makeovers in a noisy cordoned-off area. There, mere feet from bumper-to-bumper traffic, I met Sara, a distraught, 40-year-old mom who explained that her advertising agency boss was an alcoholic and that she was always left to pick up the pieces and make excuses for his erratic behavior. Sara had been enduring this for years and told stories of her boss unexpectedly canceling meetings or picking fights with employees or clients. Each time, she was the one who swooped in with the broom. She dreaded going into work each day, terrified of encountering a new mess that she would inevitably be expected to clean up. So why was she staying? She had no answer. She was wealthier, more powerful, and more accomplished in her field than Dara and Anna, but every bit as stuck.

The challenge that all of these women faced went deeper than their surface problems. Their plight was identical to that of so many women I encounter, whether it is the Olympic athlete, the Wall Street titan, the executive assistant, or the small business owner. It's a lack of confidence, a degree of paralysis, a belief that they don't have the tools to fix it, or a nagging feeling that "I do not deserve a completely full and delicious life."

Maybe you too have settled into a less than happy, less than successful life. Maybe you feel sheepish about expecting more or allowing yourself to dream. Or maybe you have a happy-ish "B+" life that could be an "awesome A" with just a few tweaks. Without the determination to have or be more, you will remain stuck in a monotonous cycle of underachieving—in life, in love, at work, and at home. Isn't it time to live up to your full potential?

Beyond the facades we put up, the clothing and hair that money can buy, so many of us are living subpar lives. We're surviving rather than thriving. We work too much and spend too little time with family and friends. We're bored, tired, and lack passion. We spend too much time thinking about the past, either waxing nostalgic or regretting our mistakes. We're unable to move two feet toward greener pastures, in part because we have no idea what direction to head in, but mainly because we're not thinking of ourselves as bakers, firmly in charge of our own recipes. Rather than forging ahead to claim the lives we want, we act like lily pads that can be pulled in any direction by the water.

I hear this on my radio show all the time. When I propose date night, a caller will express guilt about leaving her child to go out. When I mention friends, she'll laugh and say, "I remember those." When I ask how she will spend Sunday with her child, she'll claim to be too exhausted to enjoy an activity together.

We can blame our circumstances or other people for our failure to jump in the puddles and appreciate the sunsets, but in large part *we* prevent *ourselves* from doing it. We race our kids through their nightly routine of dinner, bath, bed, and book without pausing to enjoy any of it along the way. We take our child to the park but frantically look *down* at our phone the whole time, forgetting that our kids are looking *up* to us. We worry about mortgage payments and teachers' gifts and work deadlines and getting our kids off to school, but we fail to take a step back and evaluate what *our kids* see. We have dinner with an old friend but spend the whole time thinking about the work piling up as we eat. We are missing the moments, and we largely have ourselves to blame.

Guilt, the Predator

When I work with women who are stuck, their problems are bound up in feelings of guilt. When we are single, we feel guilty for not trying hard enough to meet the right person, or we regret blowing off that promising guy who showed interest five years ago. When we are married, we feel guilty for not spending any time with our friends. When we are working, we feel guilty for not being home to greet the kids after school, and while we are commuting to work we are beating ourselves up for not exercising more regularly.

When TV journalist Marlene Sanders passed away in 2015 at age 84, her son, *New Yorker* staff writer Jeffrey Toobin, was asked to talk about her and her life as a pioneer in the field and a working mother at a time when few were. Toobin described the pride he always felt for his mother's career and said, "The key to her success in both journalism and in having a family was she didn't agonize, she didn't suffer, she wasn't guilt-ridden. This was her life."[4] Sanders was not only a professional role model for her son, a successful journalist in his own right, but she also formed a tight and meaningful parental relationship with him.

Choose the Guilt-Free Life

If you choose to open up the well of guilt, you'll find that it is bottomless. The voices in our heads say, "I should be home with my child"; "I should be feeding her homemade organic meals"; "I shouldn't have stopped breast-feeding so soon"; "I should be the one at the playground with her." We are stuck in "Shouldville" instead of "Couldville." And the guilt starts early on. From the moment we become pregnant we get bombarded with questions that people don't lob at future dads. "What will you do about work after you have the baby?" "Will you cut your hours back?" "See fewer patients?" "Work from home?" It's endless. And it's just the beginning. It is easy to see how these questions from others lead us to cast doubt on our own decisions.

Guilt is dangerous; it eats up our time and drives poor decisions. When we're at work, we're underperforming because our mind is at home, agonizing over where else we "should" be. When we're at home, our families don't get the best of us because we are thinking about work. We're sleep deprived because we lie awake at night beating ourselves up. Guilt is a predator, and you can't let it be yours. When guilt begins to inform how we handle daily challenges, it becomes toxic.

Suzy Welch, former editor in chief at *Harvard Business Review*, was once hired to give a big speech to a group of insurance executives in Hawaii. As a mom of four, Suzy felt terrible about leaving her kids yet again, so she decided to bring her two little ones with her. As she explained, her goal was to balance it all, and at the time, "Every decision was based on gut or guilt."

Suzy signed up her children for a hula dancing class at the kids club so they would have something to do during her speech. The result was what became known in her family as "the jailbreak." Mid-speech, Suzy was startled to see the doors open and her two hula skirt–clad children running down the aisle toward the podium. It was at that moment she realized that the rhythm of her life was terribly off. She felt she was failing in every direction, and that something had to change.

When I first traveled for work after having kids, I was also riddled with guilt. I used to write five-page color-coded manifestos for my husband and sitter detailing every move my children needed to make in my absence, where to take them, what to feed them, and what they should wear. One day, my husband pointed out how debilitating and demotivating my color-coded pages were. "Do you realize this is not a science? Show me how you prepare their lunch and I will make it the same way." When I gave him this manifesto, I was implicitly denying that my kids were happy and safe with him, stealing his sense of autonomy. I also wasn't helping him adjust for his next time alone with the kids. He was right, and since then, my instructions have been minimal and his angst over my departure has diminished.

Once I dropped the manifesto, I also managed to drop most of the guilt. I realized that when I was away from my kids, I could be helping my family more by being as productive at work as possible. During business trips, I now try to fill every minute with a meeting, and I prioritize getting good sleep on those nights away. On top of it, I return home and proudly share stories of my trips with the kids. In that way, I feel like my short absences add to their lives rather than take away from them.

Like me, Ticketmaster chief operating officer Amy Howe transformed her relationship with guilt. When she first became a parent, guilt loomed as a daily force in her life. Over time, Amy has realized that she is a better mom and wife because she works and loves what she does. Amy has also come to see herself as a role model for her kids who get to see her working hard to earn what the family has. "I don't want my children to grow up with a sense of entitlement, so in a small way I feel like I am giving them one of the most valuable life lessons they can learn," she says.

There is a gender divide when it comes to guilt: women are typically raised to build self-esteem through relationships, while men are raised to build self-esteem through accomplishments.[5] Relying on relationships for our self-esteem is problematic because we cannot avoid disappointing others. This is the guilt trap. As anyone who has taken a guilt trip knows, the guilt path is a never-ending one. No surprise, then, that many of the 150 accomplished women I interviewed for *The Pie Life* either did not struggle with feelings of guilt or had grown to overcome them. When I asked finance executive Laura Flynn how she gives her career and her family all that she has without feeling guilty that she is shorting one or the other, she said, "I honestly don't think about it that much." You shouldn't either. Guilt is an extraneous ingredient in our pies and to reach our professional and personal potential, we are going to let go of it for good.

Juggling and Dropping

Most of us don't take control and "bake up" the delectable lives we want, but we do break out the measuring cups to determine how well we are—and aren't—doing compared with our friends and colleagues. Our dress sizes, our weights, the accomplishments of our children, the sizes of our homes, our job titles: we love to measure ourselves. We cling to almost any yardstick that is thrown our way, and most of these yardsticks are guaranteed to set us up for failure. Then we feel guilty that we aren't doing better.

Just look at the language we use to talk about our lives. Women are told we should be "jugglers." Have you Googled the image of the working mom? She's the woman holding the briefcase and the baby bottle and typing on the computer at the same time. Depressing! I have long believed that this image contributes to women leaving the workforce. It is a rare woman who can feed her child while handling a conference call—or, like Suzy Welch, who entertains her kids while putting on a business presentation. So let's agree to leave juggling to the circus professionals.

Kristen was a business development manager for a start-up. She was traveling more than she had anticipated and felt that her life was falling apart. She was missing soccer games and school plays, and most nights she couldn't make it

GOOD GUILT VERSUS BAD GUILT—A QUIZ

1. Do you second-guess yourself because of guilt?
   A. Yes
   B. No

2. Have you ever made a bad decision out of guilt?
   A. Yes
   B. No

3. Do you end up doing many things out of obligation?
   A. Yes
   B. No

4. When you leave a party, do you beat yourself up the next day over certain things you said or interactions you had?
   A. Yes
   B. No

Mostly As: Guilty
Mostly Bs: Not Guilty

home for the bedtime routine. On this Tuesday morning, she was traveling from her home in California to New York, knowing that she would miss her oldest daughter's class performance the following day. Though her husband would be there and promised to record it, she couldn't bear the idea of missing yet another event. So Kristen tortured her body a bit and took the red-eye home from New York that same evening to catch the performance.

Landing on Wednesday morning, three hours before she was supposed to be at her daughter's school, she dragged her bleary-eyed self to the office to squeeze in two hours of work before heading to the performance. Kristen lost herself in her work and was startled out of her focus by the phone ringing. It was her husband asking where she was. The performance was starting in one minute. She was a half hour away. She missed it, despite having flown all night in a coach middle seat to get there. That morning, she had done the hard part of arriving back in California and mistakenly felt like she could keep her work ball and her parenting ball in the air simultaneously. Her daughter was heartbroken because

Kristen had called her the night before to surprise her with the news that she would be there.

Kristen was on the brink of a guilt-fueled breakdown. She had tried to juggle and failed; balls were dropping everywhere. When she looks back on it now, she realizes that if she had just gotten off the plane and gone home, this entire situation would have been avoided. She hadn't gone home because she was treating herself like a bouncing ball, being tossed from one hand to the other.

Work/Life *Imbalance*

When I first entered the coaching field, I tried on many names to describe my work—work/life stylist, work/life synergy expert—but it turns out that the one term we all gather around is "work/life balance." The concept gets us into trouble because for a scale to be in perfect balance, the two sides must be equal. The metaphor of a scale makes us feel like we have to spend identical time, energy, and passion in our personal and professional lives. Anyone with a successful career knows that it is impossible to spend equal time at home and work.

Emily, a top sales executive, was distraught, telling me that she was "the worst mother." She was depressed because she was only seeing her child 10 hours a week. When I asked what she did with those 10 hours, she explained that she arrived home from work, put on her pajamas, turned off her phone, and just reveled in her daughter's presence. Emily had a thriving career, yet she had declared herself a failure and fallen into downward spirals of guilt because she was thinking about the scale. She believed that her work time and her family time each had to account for 50 percent of her waking hours, and that if they didn't, she was shorting one or the other. She had fallen into the work/life balance trap. There was no way she could be at work for fewer hours and succeed in her job, so why was she beating herself up over it? Plus, she was giving her daughter what most kids never get: daily undivided attention. Once we removed this scale image from her head and redefined her vision of success, Emily realized she could be—and already was—a great mom in just 10 hours during the workweek.

Not Having It All

In 1982, when Helen Gurley Brown, then editor of *Cosmopolitan* magazine, titled her book *Having It All*, she could hardly have anticipated that we would take that phrase and beat ourselves up with it.[6] Unfortunately, women who plant the "have it all" mantra in their minds wind up comparing their accomplishments to those of other women, and they have no trouble finding peers who appear to "have it all" more than they do. We have all done it. We see a woman standing in front of us in line at Starbucks or at the crosswalk or in the boardroom or on the playground, and we think, "She has a better life, a better body, more money, more happiness, a hotter husband, the life I want." We assume this woman is more successful, healthier, and wealthier than we are—that her life is *perfect*. Oh, and we also assume that this rich life she enjoys is utterly guilt-free.

This kind of faulty thinking leads us into spirals of guilt and jealousy. One of my favorite sayings is, "Be kind, for everyone you meet is fighting a hard battle." Life is not an à la carte menu; it is a package deal. When you get another person's treasures, you also get their troubles. If we knew a bit more about that woman's "perfect" body, we might find out that she is undergoing treatment for melanoma. If we learned more about the neighbor's incredible career, we might find out that she has been battling an employee lawsuit for three years. If we had that mom's gorgeous wardrobe, we might also have her loveless marriage. We never know about other people's lives, but what we *do* know is that nobody lives as we imagine they do. Our only path to a wonderfully satisfying life is to focus on all that *we* can do with what *we* have, baking up the best life possible for ourselves with these ingredients. We have all of the ingredients we need; we just need to shake up the recipe.

Jessica, a top executive at a major consumer products company, was always hard on herself. At work, she felt like a failure because she hadn't been promoted fast enough. When I gently reminded her that she had been the only one in her department to survive four rounds of layoffs and five bosses in eight years, she waved me off dismissively and shifted the conversation, complaining that she had not had enough time to spend cooking for her kids or to plan anything spectacular for her husband's upcoming birthday. When I reminded her that she ate dinner with her kids four nights a week, enjoyed a very tight relationship with them, and had an adoring husband, she again dismissed my point by returning back to her work woes. She bounced back and forth between beating herself up over work and her family life. She was aspiring to "have it all" and failing against an impossible measuring stick.

I once moderated a panel at NBCUniversal that featured three highly successful women executives. The audience was full of women who worked at NBC, hailing from accounts payable, human resources, production, and every other part of the company. As women filled the room, it was clear that they looked up to these three panelists, naturally assuming that they "had it all"—the giant paycheck, the impressive job title, perfect children, happy relationships. Yet that image began to unravel as soon as the panelists began talking.

I opened with a simple, unrehearsed query: "Tell us about what happened in your home *this* morning—from the moment you woke up until the moment you arrived here."

The first to respond was Amy, head of publicity. With a long bob cut and pantsuit, she looked as put together as they come. Yet what she described was a scene out of a dark comedy. That morning, she was naked and on her way into the shower when she quickly checked her e-mail and saw that a time-sensitive work crisis had erupted. Rather than tell her husband or kids what was happening, she grabbed her laptop and hid on the toilet, frantically dealing with the problem. Ten minutes later, her husband opened the door and his jaw hit the ground. "We've been looking everywhere for you . . . !" The audience howled with laughter. Perfection undone. A collective sigh of "She's just like us."

Next up was Carol, the tall, thin, blonde head of marketing who was a single mom of a 15-year-old. As her daughter was walking out the door that morning, Carol looked twice at the T-shirt she was wearing and noticed that it read, "I was raised by an iPhone." Carol begged her daughter not to wear the shirt and was firmly rebuffed. The head of marketing—she's just like us!

The women who filled the room had put these executives on a pedestal, but the moment they revealed something personal about themselves, the image of having it all evaporated. The audience allowed the panelists to rejoin us on planet Earth.

If you've been striving to have it all, I invite you to close your eyes, take a deep breath, and let that go. Does your favorite car have every feature? Did the college you attended serve every need? Does one friendship provide all of the fun, the support, and the feelings? Living a full life means living with some imperfection.

Let's Get Baking

We only get one life; it's time we made the most of it. Living devoid of passion and fulfillment is like baking a pie without the sugar. So let's throw out these three ridiculous yardsticks—juggling, balancing, and having it all—and lose the guilt too. There is no more useless ingredient, so to bake this pie, we must let it go. In the chapters that follow, we're going to develop this new way of thinking as the basis for giving you a lifestyle makeover of your own, helping you get clear on what you *really* want, with tips and strategies for living it. Let's reorganize your life by thinking about it as a pie to be savored.

My goals for you are many. I want you to leave this book:

* Feeling driven to live the best life possible
* Knowing that you deserve a great life
* Seeking out everyday enjoyment and fulfillment
* Appreciating that for life to be delicious, it needs to be a bit messy
* Abandoning the "grass is always greener" attitude
* Believing that you already have the ingredients you need for a great life
* Knowing exactly how to better manage your life
* Hearing a new voice in your head that allows you to be more present in each day
* Feeling new excitement about what lies ahead
* Appreciating that we are all in a similar boat
* Understanding how to incorporate friendship, love, fun, and community into your life

Now, you might be reading skeptically and thinking, "Yeah, right! How is all that possible?" Well, to change your life, you need both the *will* and the *way*. Let's make a deal before we begin: you provide the will and I will provide the way. If the voice in your head is saying you don't have the will, let's choose to ignore it because it is dead wrong. You have the will—we all do. Yours might be buried deep inside, but if you have picked up this book, I know you have it.

Now let's talk about the second ingredient, the way. Here is the great news. Are you ready for it?

The way is as easy as pie.

We can all change our lives. I know because I have done it in ways big and small. When I first moved to California from New York in 2011, it was chaos. My husband and I were sleep deprived (we had a 1-year-old, a 3-year-old, and a 5-year-old), overwhelmed, and had no friends or family to welcome us to our new city or ease the transition. While we were thrilled with the sudden space— the five of us had been living on top of one another in our 1,400-square-foot apartment—we were also struck by the sudden realization that we would be creating a brand new life for ourselves and it would take a ton of work. The first year post-move was an adjustment, but a few years later, I looked back and realized that all of the struggles were worth it. I want you to feel that way about the changes you are about to make.

I know change is possible for people with stagnant lives because I see meaningful change every day. When I first met Michelle Villemaire, she was a stay-at-home mom of two children, married to a TV-writer husband. Michelle told me that she planned to start a do-it-yourself (DIY) blog "one day." "When?" I asked, intentionally prompting her to repeat the timing of this plan. She confidently responded that when her youngest was in kindergarten, she would begin. It was her canned answer. She had said this a lot.

I thought of all the women I know who romanticize that time when their youngest is in kindergarten. I still do it too, claiming that I will work out regularly when my son starts kindergarten. I know a woman who plans to open a flower shop when her youngest is in kindergarten and another who plans to leave her husband when her youngest is in kindergarten.

I challenged Michelle. "Why don't you start that blog tomorrow?"

"What!" she gasped. It was as if I had recommended that she run naked down Main Street.

"Well, there is never a perfect time," I said. "And if you start six months from now, you will wish you started six months earlier. If you start tomorrow, you will wish you started yesterday."

To my amazement, Michelle decided to start her blog the very next day. As she worked on getting it off the ground, she checked in with me from time to time. She wanted to know if she should attend her first blogging conference, with whom she should network, what topics her blog should cover. What happened next to Michelle still excites me. Within the space of only a year, she had changed her life and her outlook. She grew her blog, was invited to be a contributor to many big media platforms, and eventually landed herself on a TLC show. And she has even greater moments coming in what I know will be a long and successful career.

By the way, her youngest is still not in kindergarten. *What if she had waited?*

Michelle accomplished so much prompted by just a tiny push. Chances are, that's all you need too—that and some tricks for managing your time better, strengthening your relationships, and making your daily life a little easier. Don't settle for a half-baked life, and don't wait. A desire to thrive runs deep inside all of us. The key is to learn how to become your own baker—to mix and shake up the ingredients until your life is as rich and delicious as possible.

Let's envision your life as a pie, and in the next chapter, let's start imagining your flavor.

Taking a step back and asking ourselves whose voice we are hearing can help us to stop listening to it. Is it the voice of your own mother who thinks you should be home with the kids, like she was? Is it the voice of your boss who never had kids and makes you feel like you don't work hard enough no matter how much you do? Is it the voice of your husband who compares you to his do-no-wrong sister-in-law? Is it the voice of your friend who downplays your career? Or at the end of the day, is it an image you created in your mind and refuse to let go of? Identifying the voice is the first step to ignoring it.

THE VOICES INSIDE YOUR HEAD: AN EXERCISE

1. When you hear disapproval, whose voice do you hear?
   A. I don't hear disapproval
   B. Your spouse or parents
   C. Many people
   D. Yourself

2. When someone questions your choice, you:
   A. Wonder why you ever asked them
   B. Consider what they are saying
   C. Will never be impacted
   D. Change your decision

3. When you make a decision, you:
   A. Stick with it
   B. Agonize over it but only occasionally change it
   C. Change your mind like the wind
   D. I prefer that others make a decision

Scoring: If you have less than two As, you need to work on trusting yourself and gaining confidence in your instincts and decision-making.

CHAPTER TWO

PIE IN THE SKY

As soon as I accomplish one thing, I just set a higher goal. That's how I've gotten to where I am.

— BEYONCÉ

If you have picked up this book, I would bet your ambitions and dreams are not all that they can be. But I have big dreams for you. This is the moment where we are going to reimagine your life. We'll develop a "pie in the sky" vision for everything your life can be—all of its potential. One of my favorite things about dreams is that anyone can have them. They don't cost anything, they don't render judgments, they don't bite back, and they don't hurt. To the contrary, they can motivate us to take action, they give us purpose, they help us set goals, and they make us feel great.

For most of your life other people have probably fed you goals. When you were in high school, your goal was to get into college. When you graduated from college, your goal was to find a job, then to move up in your career, get married, have kids, buy a house . . . and let's stop here. Many of us stop thinking of personal goals once we get pregnant or reach a certain point in adulthood. For the first time and without even realizing it, we are goal-less. You used to be a master goal setter. Then, post-child, your spotlight suddenly shifted away from you and onto your children. Suddenly, their goals—getting them into school and launching them into their lives—were the only ones that mattered. But it is critically important not to confuse these parenting goals with your own personal goals.

Goals keep us alive; they make life worth living. When my friend Laurie David discovered Peggy Freydberg's poetry, Peggy was 106 years old. Peggy had not started writing poetry until she turned 90, and had never expected her poems to be turned into a published work. When Peggy died at age 107, Laurie said it was as though she had waited for her book to be published before she passed. We hear stories like this a lot—people holding onto life until meeting their daughter's baby for the first time, or achieving some sort of milestone.

My dad's father, William Ettus, was a happy and gentle man. When he had a stroke at age 79, he was taken to the hospital and was completely unresponsive. When my dad entered the room later that day, William locked eyes with my father and a single tear streamed down his face. Almost immediately after, he died. It sounds like a dramatic moment from a movie, but it's not. He had waited to see his only child one last time.

To really seize all of your energy and potential, you need goals. Just like a company will never reach the height of productivity without a clear mission statement, you will never thrive without goals. *What are your goals? What do you dream of? Where do you want to go?* Let's figure it out together by creating your personal vision statement.

Visioning

Imagine that you're entering a beautiful kitchen, and you have all of the cooking tools you need to bake a pie. The oven is preheating, and you're getting ready to gather the key ingredients. But before you do, you have to decide what kind of pie you're making.

I love asking rooms full of women to imagine their flavors. When I do, I am really asking them to craft a vision of what their lives *could* be. So few of us take the time to envision the life we want. We live our lives passively according to messages we've absorbed from the media, our parents and friends, or our cultures. My favorite educator, Sir Ken Robinson, once said, "The best evidence of human creativity is the life we've created for ourselves." It is true. We have more power over how our lives unfold than anyone else in the universe. But in order to create our lives, we must first frame a vision of where we want to be.

Your life can be radically different from the one you live today. It could go from being a crumb cake to a decadent coconut crème pie. Or it could be just a variation on the theme, a pie filled with cherries instead of strawberries. What life do *you* want to live? Do you want a more exotic life with more travel to faraway places? Do you want a bigger, better career? A fuller, more satisfying social life? A life that lets you spend more time with your family, or that frees up more time for your hobbies? More emotional intimacy, or a more active sex life? Let's define the general contours of what the future life of your dreams will look like.

Once we do that, we can delve deeper into the slices of your pie and develop ways to get you where you want to go.

If you could choose any flavor pie to describe you and your life at its best, what would yours be? Mine would be chocolate cream: soft yet crunchy, sweet, decadent, and messy. You might choose peach or cherry. My friend from New York likes to think of her life as a pizza pie, and a woman from Australia calls hers meat pie. Whatever your flavor, from this day forward I want you to kick every other baker out of your kitchen and claim it as your own. You are in charge of your own pie; only you get to decide what it will look and taste like.

Risk manager Catina D'Achille of Oklahoma thinks of her life as a dark berry pie. "It's sweet with a hint of tartness. It fits my personality: go-getter, professional attire/dark dress, but I can be a spitfire and when you least expect it, I surprise you. Hence the tartness." For Texas-based LaNae Kelley, a medical office manager, her life is lemon meringue. "It is refreshing and rich, enough tart to make your face tighten up and look silly, with sweet moments thrown in between." New York–based marketing executive Sally Susman sees her best life as a pecan pie "because it's dense, sweet, and salty. Essentially old fashioned." And it's a delicious salted caramel pie for New York television producer Koyalee Chanda: "Mostly sweet, but every once in a while, you get hit with a sharp taste of reality."

If you aren't a big pie eater, picture your favorite layer cake or turn your beloved blueberry muffin into a pie. No need to get too literal. Plus there is an upcoming exercise that will walk you through it even further.

An Array of Visions

In thinking about what kind of life you want to lead, it helps to understand what your options are. Let's get a fuller sense of what's possible for you by meeting several women and comparing the very different visions they have crafted for their lives. Each of these women once felt terribly stuck or unhappy. Yet each took charge of her life, rewrote her recipe, and baked a pie that she now finds wholesome, delicious, and satisfying.

The Outsider in the Big City

Meet Alex, a 43-year-old artist with one child who is married to a musician. Alex lives in upstate New York, where she and her family have a close-knit set of friends, a quiet and relaxing lifestyle that involves healthy eating and cooking, lots of family time, and a wonderful dose of the arts and nature mixed in. Alex and her family travel a fair amount together, and Alex has sacrificed some of her career ambitions for a peaceful life she loves.

But it wasn't always this way. At age 33, Alex was single and living in Brooklyn, working at her art career and tolerating the grind of the city. She had grown up with a fast-paced life, but it didn't suit her. Alex took a solo trip to attend a friend's wedding in Canada and decided to show up three days early to explore. She met a couple of people on the airplane there and when she bumped into them the next day, they invited her to brunch. Fortunately, she said yes. (Good things tend to happen when we are open to new experiences.) It was at this chance brunch that Alex met her future husband, who was on his way to tour with a band throughout Europe. The two kept in touch and started dating upon his return to the United States. They very deliberately mapped out a life together, bought land in upstate New York, and made it happen. *Alex envisioned it and now she is living it.*

The Ambitious Educator

Meet Sheri, a Los Angeles resident in her mid-thirties who has two children and is aiming for a third. She also has a very successful career as vice president of a private elementary school, has a great nanny whom she counts on as a partner in raising the kids, and a husband in his sixth and final year of graduate school. Sheri spends her vacations and most evenings with her kids, has a wide circle of friends, and feels like she and her husband are building a big life together.

But it wasn't always this way. Sheri had once been a teacher. Although she loved working in education, she quickly recognized that her future options were limited. Sheri wanted a role where she could reach hundreds of students and families at the same time—something a traditional teaching position couldn't offer—so she took on a job in development (a.k.a. fundraising), opening herself up to a business and administrative role. Within two years she was offered a job as head of admissions at her old school, a position for which she would not have been qualified had she not taken that development job. On the child-care front, she hired a new nanny who could become part of the family. This closeness gave her more flexibility over her schedule, serving her well as she ascends in her career. *She envisioned it and now she is living it.*

The Happy Divorcee

Meet Margot, a 45-year-old who runs a major PR firm in Dallas. She's also a single mom of three and dates a successful man who has two kids of his own. The two plan to marry and in anticipation of this, Margot already functions as a stepmom to her fiancé's kids. Because Margot is focused on continuously building her business, she must go out most nights of the week to attend networking and client events. Still, she always stops at home beforehand to spend at least an hour or two with her kids, a practice that has enabled her to build and keep a very close relationship with them. Margot also has a jam-packed social life, with tons of friends and fun.

But it wasn't always this way. Following her divorce, Margot was lonely, overwhelmed, and anxious about her children's happiness and sense of security. She wanted to be in a new, healthy relationship, preferably with a man who was already a father; she wanted to help her kids thrive amidst personal turmoil; and she wanted to see her business continue to grow and secure her family's financial future. To make that all happen, Margot spent a year dating once or twice a week until she met the man she now considers her soul mate. Understanding the importance of a stable, regular routine in her children's lives, she began her practice of coming home for an hour or two each evening. She was intentional about maintaining her social life and her new relationship, both areas that have always been important to her. *She envisioned it and now she is living it.*

The Independent Consultant

Meet Mary, a single mom of one child who splits her time between New York and Philadelphia. Mary is enrolled in a doctorate program, which she believes will help further her career as an organizational change consultant. Because she is momming, working, or studying, she has no time right now for romance in her life. That's fine—Mary feels great about her current path, finding tremendous joy in her son, in her work, and in her studies.

But it wasn't always this way. For many years, Mary languished in a bad marriage. She wasn't suffering any abuse, but Mary realized that her marriage to an unhappy and unmotivated man posed an unmanageable threat to her own success and happiness. Mary felt empty returning home from work each night to a passionless and loveless relationship. She had always been super driven, yet now she realized that marrying someone with as little ambition as her husband had stunted her own career. After years of thought, Mary bravely initiated her divorce. Once the dust settled, both she and her ex became great co-parents to their one child. Her new independence also gave her the strength to go after her dream of getting a doctorate in her field. *She envisioned it and now she is living it.*

Here, then, are examples of four very different women living lives they love, ones they deliberately designed for themselves. If you look at their lives, they didn't necessarily choose the easiest paths, but they maneuvered their way to a better life even if there were speed bumps along the way.

What sacrifices might you need to make to get to a life you love? Are there elements of these women's lives that appeal to you? Which of these women do you most identify with and why?

Your Pie Life

With these stories in mind, let's now work together to write your vision. It's easy and fun, so find a comfortable spot and your favorite beverage, and start filling in the blanks!

1. If you were to describe the you of your dreams, she would feel . . .
    Use three adjectives. For each one, write a line explaining why you chose it.

    _____

    _____

    _____

2. How does your dream life compare with your existing life?
    A. I would spend MORE time in the following areas:
    B. I would spend LESS time in the following areas:
    Consider elements such as career, children, partner, friends, hobbies, etc., and please explain your answers to (A) and (B).

    _____

    _____

    _____

3. You would create a home that looked like . . .
    Think of where your home would be located geographically, its general atmosphere, how neat it would be, how messy, the décor, and so on. What

special features would it have? How does it compare with what your home looks like now?

_____

_____

_____

4. Your relationship would look like . . .
   Describe your dream relationship in some detail. Does it feature mutual love and respect? Are you sharing responsibilities at home and with the kids? Are you together all the time, or do you each enjoy alone time? Is there a lot of romance? More meaningful conversations? More date nights? How does it compare with your current relationship?

_____

_____

_____

5. Your parenting style would be . . .
   Describe in some detail what kind of parent you'd be, and how it would be different from your parenting today. Would you be warmer? More engaged? More structured? Would you spend more time having fun? Would you build more traditions? Would you be more or less like your own parents?

_____

_____

_____

6. Your social life would be . . .
   Describe your dream social life in some detail. Would it be more active? Would you entertain more? Would you have a broader circle of friends? Would you have fewer but closer relationships? Would you reconnect with old friends from your past? Would you travel more with friends?

_____

_____

_____

7. Your health regimen would include . . .
    Describe in some detail what your health activities would be in the life of your dreams. Would you sleep more? Work out more? Obsess less over your weight? Eat better? Attend doctors' appointments more regularly? Go to therapy? Drink less? Meditate? Try out new forms of exercise?

    _____

    _____

    _____

8. If there's one thing you need more of in your life, it is . . .
    Think about one thing that is most missing from your life today. Might it be more fun, more time for your career, more time with kids, more intimacy? Why is this element important to you? Why is it lacking right now, and how does the absence of it make you feel?

    _____

    _____

    _____

9. If there's one thing in your existing life that you would keep in your dream life, it would be . . .
    As dissatisfied as we might be with our existing lives, many things might be worth keeping, albeit with tweaks or adjustments. What is one thing about your life that you simply love and wouldn't want to lose? Why do you love it? How does it make you feel?

    _____

    _____

    _____

10. Here's a fun one. If you had to associate your life with the flavor of a pie, what would it be and why?
    Would it be sweet or savory? Rich and decadent, or light and refreshing? Would it be fruity? Chocolatey? Please explain your answer.

    _____

    _____

    _____

Now let's put your responses together. Once you compile your vision, you might find that it seems a bit unruly, sprawling across several pages. If so, edit it down a little, taking out the superfluous thoughts while retaining your core ideas. Let it sit for a few minutes, and then come back to it and edit it down some more. Keep editing until you have a single, beautiful page, short enough to keep you focused, but detailed enough to encompass your entire pie. This is your manageable and achievable vision.

Imagining Your Recipe

Now that you have identified the flavor of your pie and the life you want to lead, it's time to start thinking about the recipe—in other words, *how* you might move from your current life to a life you *love*. The life of our dreams won't just magically pop into being simply because we've imagined it. We need to take steps to move toward this life.

Our lives fall into six or seven slices. They are:

* Career
* Children (This slice may or may not be in your pie.)
* Health
* Relationship (or quest to find one)
* Community
* Friends
* Hobbies

Each of these slices is worthy of your goals individually, but this is a case where blending can become destructive. Without compartmentalization of your slices, your life becomes an unruly pile of dough and ingredients. Once you split your pie into slices, your life will suddenly feel far more manageable. I want you to pursue your goals for each slice independently. Sure, they might overlap sometimes, but by looking at them individually, you will perceive them as far more achievable.

For example, picture your to-do list. If you focused on hiring a new sales star and buying holiday gifts in the same breath, you would drown in a sea of to-dos and nothing would ever get done. But when you tackle your items one at a time and in pieces—e.g., for the next hour, I will focus on personal errands, or for the next hour I will work on my presentation for work—these items become goals that you carry to the finish line.

Easy as Pie

The idea of big change can feel daunting. But as Amy's story will show you, even small changes can yield dramatic results. Amy was 38 years old, exhausted, and just barely holding it all together before she wrote out her vision. A Cincinnati resident who worked as a mid-level marketing manager, she had her hands full with her job, her three kids, and her husband. She had been a college athlete but now had no time to work out. Intimacy with her husband? A nonstarter. Amy was on a daily treadmill, and she saw no possibility of escape. At my urging, and after a bit of hesitation, Amy sat down and wrote her "pie in the sky" vision. Her list included unhurried morning breakfasts with the kids, time to hit the gym a few days a week and get back in shape, more intimacy with her husband, and more day trips with the kids. Her vision was a far stretch from her reality, but with some small changes I knew we could get her there.

To start, Amy spoke to her husband about carving out time for them both to work out. They shifted lunch making and picking out clothes to the night before so they could take turns going to the gym or driving the kids to school in the morning. They carved out a weekly date night and committed to going to sleep at the same time together at least four nights a week. They planned out day trips at the beginning of each month. Within just one week, their kids felt the impact of these small changes. The workouts and preparation the night before eased the stress on Amy and her husband, and as a result, mornings became a relative breeze. Their entire home felt lighter.

You can make similar progress. Now that you have your vision, print it out, post it on your bulletin board or your bathroom mirror, and start reading it daily. If you are partnered or your kids are teenagers or older, consider sharing it with them too. The first step in turning your dreams into reality is to give those dreams a tangible life of their own. Print them and they start existing. Talk about them and they start breathing. Take steps to reaching them and they start forming. And now that your dreams are in place, it's time to get slicing.

CHAPTER THREE

SLICING YOUR PIE

If you look at what you have in life, you'll always have more. If you look at what you don't have in life, you'll never have enough.

— OPRAH WINFREY

When Jada, a Chicago attorney, came to me, she was flipping out. She'd had a massive fight with her husband, her son was being bullied at school, her mom was sick, her cat was on his last legs, and her company was in the middle of layoffs. Put together, this list of calamities would make any of us want to throw in the towel. But I knew that if we looked at her life slice by slice, it would suddenly appear manageable. So we did.

If we evaluate our lives without giving them an underlying structure, we tend to focus on what isn't working, not about what is. But life looks differently when we conceive of it as a pie made up of slices. Even if we worry about our parents and our children and our business, we're also forced to look at slices where things are going great. We find that we've never been in better physical shape, for instance, or that we have a great group of friends. We naturally bake gratitude right into our pies, and that makes everything seem easier.

In Jada's case, health was a strong area. As she told me, "I have been eating well and working out three days a week. I feel great about my progress." (The health slice hadn't made her original list of things to talk to me about because nothing was wrong there, and like all people who feel overwhelmed in their lives, Jada only poured her worries on the table rather than including the slices that were going well.) When it came to Jada's career, things weren't so bad either. "Layoffs are happening," she said, "but I have survived them before and I have strengthened my network and have great experience. I will get my resume together just in case." As for Jada's children slice, she revealed that her daughter was thriving, yet her son had serious issues. But this time, now that we were looking at each slice on its own, Jada proposed some potential solutions without prodding from me. She decided she would talk to her son's teachers and at the same time encourage his friendships with the kids on his swim team outside of school.

We went through each of Jada's seven slices and focused on the ones that weren't working and also the ones that were. When we looked at her life this way, it was impossible for Jada not to feel a degree of appreciation for what was going right. This perspective led to gratitude for all that was going well and boosted her energy to handle all the areas that were not.

The Slice Is Right

Slicing is the key to achieving the productivity and happiness you are seeking. It allows you to feel a sense of control over your life. And it works on a number of levels. For instance, when we think of our life as a pie made up of slices, we are able to break free of unhealthy "work/life balance" thinking. We've seen that the notion of work/life balance fails us by suggesting that there is a "perfect" balance to be had, and that something is wrong with us if we can't sustain it. But work/life balance also dooms us to fail because of the unrealistic notions about time it contains. In our misguided conception, the properly balanced work/life day looks something like: life—work—life. But a successful life doesn't look like that. It involves going to the gym during your lunch hour; having friends over on Sunday nights so that you can see them *and* spend time with your kids; checking e-mails after you put the kids to bed; or having your spouse meet you at the tail end of your business trip so that you can sneak in a night away together. The real pattern of our life is more like work—life—life—work—work—work—life—life—work—life, and it varies daily.

Just acknowledging this change to the work/life framework is not enough; we also need to realize that work is only one of the six or seven slices of your life. Real life involves community and friends and a relationship (or the quest to find one) and children (if you choose to have them) and health and hobbies and a career. As you adjust to the realization that many slices are involved, you can see that the pattern might look like this: children—work—friends—work—health—work—children—relationship—work. When you expect that every day of your life might include a combination of career, children, health, relationship, community, friends, and hobbies, each day becomes a refreshing back and forth between your slices. You have a new way to navigate your day, not to mention a set of building blocks for building a beautiful and full life.

When I was writing this book, there were so many days when it felt like work—work—work. If I had the image in my head of life—work—life, I would be beating myself up every day over the dramatic delta between what it should have been and what it was. But because I realize that real life is never perfectly balanced every day, I can still give myself permission to go to my friend's birthday party or a date night even on a day when I have been working and haven't seen my kids. Because the next day I will find a way to make it a little more kids—work—kids. That is the thing about the pie—it is mine to bake, and now it is yours too.

Over time, you too will find that slicing changes the voice in your head. When your babysitter doesn't show to pick up your child from school and you are in the middle of a meeting at work, your old voice would say, "There goes life getting in the way of work again. Something isn't right about my life." Your new voice, on the other hand, will reflect your acceptance that life is by nature a bit messy—that work and the other slices of your life are not separated by a velvet rope. In fact, they're all meant to be eaten, and sometimes you swallow one bite just seconds before the other one lands on your plate. Inflexibly thinking of a day as "devoted exclusively to the kids" or "devoted to work" is what gets you into trouble. Accepting the idea that you will be going back and forth between your slices allows you to ease the pressure and drop the guilt.

In her moving *Observer* article about dating as a suddenly single mom of three who found herself alone after 23 years with her ex-husband, writer Deborah Copaken describes, "One minute you're getting a text from your inappropriately young Tinder date . . . the next you're digging through a public trash can for a diorama shoebox for your kid."[7] Deborah's expectation that the slices of her life will come in rapid succession and often overlap, helps her embrace and enjoy the happy chaos. Fulfillment is born from the messiness. We all should embrace this outlook. When you remove the "I can't believe . . ." from your reaction to life's challenges, you eradicate the groaning tone in your head and allow yourself to welcome life's vagaries. At times they will be funny, at others aggravating, overwhelming, or exhilarating. Anticipate that these challenges will always exist and appreciate them, because fighting the inevitable is exhausting and self-defeating.

Identifying Your Slices

Understandably, figuring out which areas of your life are significant enough to warrant a slice can feel completely overwhelming and send you into a spiral of anxiety. Is church a slice? Is my dog a slice? My computer class? I have two jobs and I go to school part-time. Do they each get a slice?

You don't need to do two years of research or travel the world to find out. Here are the ingredients that go into the slices we've discussed; you will see that each of your activities falls into one of them:

Career

Every minute that you spend at the office or answering e-mails from home or attending classes toward your degree or networking or job searching—this is all part of your career slice. What are the forces that have shaped how much time you spend in this category? It might be the economic reality of making ends meet, or your need to pursue your family vision, or the demands of building your career and moving ahead. Or your desire to feel fulfilled. Or the goal of serving as a role model to your children.

Children

If you have kids, the forces determining how much time you spend here are self-evident. Your child wakes up at the crack of dawn? So do you. She is home sick or needs to be dropped off? That's your responsibility. There are playdates and doctors' appointments to schedule and birthday parties to plan. You need to spend time together as a family. But as a working parent, you are not aiming to win the face-time game. The best parenting comes through connecting. While there may not be much you can do to change the overall amount of time allotted to this category, you can spend your time with your kids differently—and we will discuss this in a later chapter.

Health (and Self-Care)

Your sleep, your fitness routine, your nutrition, your beauty, style, and grooming regimen all fall under health and self-care. If you get weekly manicures, they belong in here, as do the hours you sleep and the time you spend at the hair salon or the gym or the doctor. What forces are driving your allotment here? Maybe you feel miserable when you don't work out, or you watched your mom die of heart disease so you spend extra time cooking nutritious meals or monitoring your blood pressure. For most of us, health is a nonnegotiable allocation of time essential to making us feel good.

Relationship

If you are single, this category includes everything involved in your quest to find a partner—setting up an online profile, dating, going out, late nights when you find someone you like, you name it. Or maybe you're just happily single and choosing to spend this time having fun on the dating scene. If you are coupled or married, the texture of this slice is different; it includes time spent together and all that is involved in nurturing your relationship and growing and celebrating your connection. If you are engaged, it could include wedding planning.

Community

Whether it is church or school or your town, you likely maintain some connection to a larger community. If you don't, it's time to start. All of your volunteering and religious activities fall into this category. If you are on the community board, the library committee, or the PTA, or you're the coach of your child's soccer team, you are engaged in your community too. Building community, maintaining one, and participating in one takes time.

Friends (and Extended Family)

It is not selfish to have friends when you are a busy working parent; it is essential. And it isn't only friendships that deserve your time; it is relationships with your siblings, parents, nieces, nephews, godchildren, and pets. For your sanity and emotional fulfillment, for the happiness of your children and more, you need to spend time on these relationships.

Hobbies

This slice is for the marathon runners or the knitters, the readers, the gardeners, the sailors, the crafters, or the tennis players. Spending time on a hobby might sound like a pipe dream to you, but the Pie Life will get you to a place where you have time for one. Your ability to pursue hobbies might be somewhat limited—it could just be a sliver in your pie, at least until the kids or your career don't need as much of your time.

Out of Your Control

Now that we've identified the slices, it's important to think of them in helpful ways. A lot of the tension you experience every day might come from feeling you should be slicing your time differently. You wish that you spent less time at work or more time on your fitness or with your spouse or kids or visiting your dad in his elder care facility. This is guilt, the predator, invading your mind. Katie Hood, CEO of the One Love Foundation, a nonprofit that combats campus relationship violence, explains, "Every day involves flipping between multiple roles—wife, mom, friend, CEO—and frequently feeling guilty or incompetent about all of the oscillations."

There's no reason to feel guilty. First, our slices will change over time in ways we can't control. A sick parent or child, for instance, can abruptly force a change in our time allocation. So can a new relationship. As a single mom of Jake and founder of BlogHer, Lisa Stone had adjusted to her busy lifestyle. When she met the love of her life, Chris, who had two kids of his own, a number of things became easier, including her work travel, because her partner was there to care for Jake. But she also found her time disappearing. As Lisa explained to me, the hour after Jake went to bed no longer belonged to her, but to her relationship. And it wasn't just that; she also lost the time she had dedicated to running. "I gave up being an athlete for my relationship, but now my heart and emotional muscles are in better shape than I ever thought possible," Lisa reflected. Her circumstances were dictating the slices of her pie. She really didn't have that much wiggle room, but she was finding ways to make her new life work as successfully as possible.

We also determine our slices by making decisions that reflect important goals, desires, or values. In Katie's case, she and her husband chose to live in Bronxville, a suburb of New York with a great public school. This means that her husband commutes to his demanding job at an investment bank in New York City, which takes time. Katie and her husband dreamed of having a large family, so they chose to have four children, which also takes time. Katie battled postpartum depression and returning to work helped her to overcome it. Katie loves her important and demanding job at One Love Foundation, and she loves her four children and her husband. There isn't much she would change about those circumstances—she chose them: her geography, her spouse, the number of children, her career. Yet she is still beating herself up over the allocation of her time each day.

If Katie were to embrace the idea that her slices are sensible, she could emancipate herself from her daily guilt. If she worked less, she couldn't be as successful at her job, and if she spent less time on her kids and her marriage, they would suffer too. She is being rational about the division of her time. So what can she give up? The guilt. There is no perfect answer to how we should be living our lives. We all have independent constraints and strengths, histories and conditions that led us to where we are today. By realizing that rational choices we've made have affected our slices, and that the pain points in our pies are often there for good reason, we can drop the guilt and live our days a whole lot lighter. As I like to say, the "slice is right!"

Messy Moments

It is 11:31 a.m. and you are in the midst of preparing for a big presentation with your boss when you get a call from your daughter's school saying that she is sick. Instantly, your world feels like it is crumbling and you start questioning your life choices, still thinking of yourself as a failed juggler with balls dropping all around you. At this moment it is hard to see that you have made these choices rationally, and that your pie looks the way it does for good reason.

This is not the time to question your choices, but rather to accept that life gets messy, and this is a messy moment. It will pass and your life will return to its natural equilibrium once your child gets better and the presentation is complete. Making more of this moment would be like trying to talk to your child about his sadness in the middle of a tantrum. Empathize with yourself until the messy moment passes, at which point you will have the perspective to reflect on it rationally. This is also not a moment for guilt. It is a time to accept that life is imperfect and the more you can turn it into a story along the way rather than a story that levels you on the way, the quicker you will get through it.

The Sizes: A Pie Life Exercise

Now that we've introduced the slices, let's get a visual sense of what your pie *currently* looks like, so that we can figure out what you *want* it to look like. To start, we will divide each slice based on how much time it consumes for you right now. Seeing how big each slice is can help us understand where your life is currently falling short, and where opportunities might exist to tweak the recipe so that you can lead a life that you love. We acknowledge again that you have probably made very deliberate choices for your life. The point here is not to judge yourself, but to gain new perspective on the life you currently have, so that we can implement changes to make it even better.

Let's pair your seven categories with your week and write down how many hours you spend each day on each category. Now translate that to percentages, and if there is anything atypical about this week (e.g., you took two days off from work, or it is the last week of school; or your mom is visiting from St. Louis), please adjust the hours back to what a typical week would look like before calculating your percentages.

	Mon	Tue	Wed	Thur	Fri	Sat	Sun
Career							
Children							
Health & Self-Care							
Relationship							
Community							
Friends & Family							
Hobbies							

Your pie will look something like this:

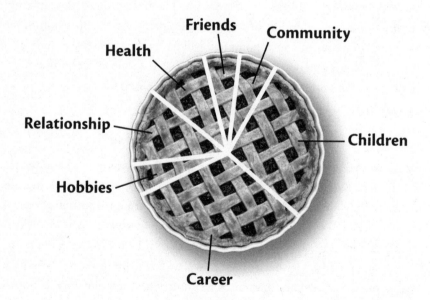

The Pie Life

Building Your New Pie

Now that you've mapped out your existing pie, let's set goals to help you reconfigure your slices—it's a critical step in moving toward the delicious life you *want*. Right now, your slices are competing for your time and energy; that will change once we define goals for each slice. You'll find yourself bouncing back and forth more flexibly between your slices: some days one slice gets weight over another, and on other days they are more evenly divided. By setting your slice-specific goals, you will no longer be focused on the time you don't have or feel guilty about your aimlessness. To the contrary, you will feel energized once you set new goals for each area of your life and focus on them.

Think about your present life. Do you have goals that propel you out of bed each morning? Many of us don't, and we compensate by adopting our kids' goals as our own or, even worse, projecting goals onto our children: "Her team will get to the finals." "He will get straight As." "She will be class president." This kind of pressure engenders a fear of failure in children and actually backfires—your drive causes them to lack motivation.[8] When we afflict children with our own hopes and dreams, we stifle their futures rather than guide them. If you find yourself looking in inappropriate places for a sense of purpose, it's time to return to goals—*yours*.

The New Year's Resolution Trap

Of course, there are goals—and there are *goals*. Crafting them in the right way makes all the difference. Let's talk for a moment about something I call the "New Year's resolution trap." It's December. You are getting ready for the holidays and buying teacher gifts, planning a festive get-together for the extended family, choosing presents for the kids, packing for vacation, and wrapping things up at work. Amidst the frenzy, you realize that your pants aren't fitting the way they used to. So you decide that you must lose 40 pounds. With the New Year approaching, you insist that losing weight will be the perfect New Year's resolution. Since you're not starting the diet until the New Year, you allow yourself to eat whatever you want on your vacation in the final two weeks before the diet begins.

You have just fallen into the New Year's resolution trap. You make some giant goal and fail to keep it because it is unrealistic. You're not alone; by June, 54 percent of New Year's resolutions are abandoned.[9] Why is this happening? Because people make grand, unachievable goals that they can't possibly live up to, rather than taking small steps to change their lifestyles. But we won't let that happen to your goals anymore; by recognizing the pitfalls, we are going to avoid the traps.

The most popular New Year's resolution is losing weight. Yet a whopping 95 percent of dieters eventually regain the weight they lose. Why are all these people torturing themselves? As a would-be dieter, if you make small lifestyle changes instead of dramatic deprivations, you will achieve greater success. According to Dr. James Beckerman, cardiologist and author of *The Flex Diet*, "The two most effective behaviors for losing weight are to weigh yourself daily (and write it down), and keep a food diary." Even with a goal as hard to tackle as weight loss, it's the small changes that stick.

Choosing Your Goals

During the first part of your life, you may have pursued goals that other people proposed—the college admission you were told to shoot for, the marriage proposal your parents expected. Now it is time to set the goals that *you* care about, to take a hard look at the "pie in the sky" vision statement you created and make your own goals for each slice. We want to choose achievable goals that can impact your life immediately. Let's avoid the broad goals like "lose 20 pounds" that leave us destined to fall short and focus on manageable ones like "eat dessert only twice a week." We want to make lifestyle changes that stick. You will know you have picked the right goals if you feel eager to achieve them and find it easy to come up with concrete action steps that will get you there. You will feel excited to go for your goals and feel zero sense of dread.

Let's begin by looking back at our seven slices: career, children, health, relationship, community, friends, and hobbies. To help you, I have put together some sample goals for each slice. Pick up your pen and, as you look at these possible goals, circle any of them that feel like they will get you closer to your "pie in the sky" vision statement from chapter 2. We will probe deeper into your slices later on; this is the time to heat the oven.

Let's start with health because in many ways this is the most tangible of all the categories. As we defined it, health encompasses sleep, any relaxation or exercise regimen, doctors' appointments, and self-care, including any time you spend on beauty and style. Note the difference between these overly broad goals and the more achievable ones:

Broad: Get more sleep
Achievable: Go to bed by 11:00 p.m. each night
Broad: Work out
Achievable: Go cycling three times per week

Here are some more sample health goals that are likely achievable (although not necessarily easy):

- Go to boxing class three days per week
- Only eat ice cream on weekends
- Reduce weekly sugar intake by 30 percent
- Schedule regular beauty appointments
- Take two long walks each weekend
- Spend more time outside each day
- Schedule checkups at the doctor
- Leave my office for a 15-minute walk every afternoon
- Limit myself to one glass of wine each night

Now we go to your career. Because you spend so much time on this slice and there are a wide variety of possibilities, let's keep the goals as specific as possible:

Broad: Earn more money
Achievable: Ask for a raise
Broad: Build my network
Achievable: Reach out to three new contacts each week

Sample career goals might include:

- Ask for a promotion once I exceed sales goals for three consecutive months
- Build my network with three new contacts per month
- Make more interdepartmental relationships by adding a new lunch each week

- Take on a new project at work
- Ingratiate myself with my coworkers over a series of coffee dates
- Start working on my new business idea every Saturday morning
- Add three new hires to my business
- Reach new sales goals
- Update my social media profiles

When it comes to finding a relationship, you want to be as specific as possible about your action steps. As for nurturing an existing relationship, you want to think about time spent together as well as larger goals.

Broad: Find a partner
Achievable: Create an online dating profile
Broad: Improve communication
Achievable: Find 20 minutes each day to check in with my partner

Here are some sample relationship goals:

- Post my online dating profile
- Go on two new dates a week
- Spend 20 minutes each evening talking with my partner
- Have sex at least two times per week
- Call my partner to say hi each afternoon
- Buy tickets to a theater series for me and my partner
- Plan a yearly vacation without the kids

With the children slice, we tend to get overwhelmed by broad goals like spending more time with them and connecting more. When you get more specific, you will reduce your guilt and improve your relationship with your kids. Small, tangible tweaks will make big differences.

Broad: Spend more quality time with the kids
Achievable: Plan a weekly "date" with each child—even if it is only a 30 minute walk or a trip to get ice cream
Broad: Get my kids to listen to me

Achievable: Spend time each night lying next to my children and talking (the more connected kids feel, the more they listen)

Here are some potential goals in the children slice:

- Plan meaningful weekend activities with the kids
- Get to know my child's teachers
- Have family dinner at least four nights a week
- Map out weekly meals in advance
- Make it to two sports games a month
- Expose the kids to less of my stress by turning off the tech from 7:00 to 9:00 p.m.
- Teach my son to ride a bike
- Add an extra 15 minutes for a relaxing bedtime routine
- Plan a family trip
- Eliminate all phones during meals

Friend time includes time with your sister or your cousins or any relationship that includes adult friendship. This might not seem like an obvious category for goal setting, but when you neglect this slice, you will watch it shrink down to nothing. When you nurture this slice, your friendships will be more reliable and rewarding.

Broad: Be a better friend
Achievable: Make one phone call each week to an old friend
Broad: Spend more time with my sister
Achievable: Visit my sister at least two times per month

Here are potential goals in the friendship slice:

- Plan a dinner party
- Get in touch with one old friend every Tuesday
- Start a monthly board game night
- Keep my phone off the dinner table when out with friends
- Start a book club

- When friends ask how I am, really tell them
- Make two new parent friends at my child's school
- Make time for lunch with one new friend each month
- Invite family over for a monthly Sunday night dinner
- Call family or close friends on their birthdays

As we will discuss in chapter 12, your community is an essential part of your successful lifestyle—but it takes work to get it right. This is where the goals come into play.

Broad: Volunteer less
Achievable: Select one activity to commit to each year
Broad: Get to know my neighbors
Achievable: Engage neighbors in conversations beyond the weather

Here are some sample goals for the community slice:

- Pare down volunteering to one commitment at a time
- Volunteer for one committee at each child's school
- Invite the neighbors for Thursday night drinks
- Get involved in a club at my church
- Run for a position on my local community board
- Attend a political event every three months
- Learn about my local politicians
- Pick a cause and get active in its local charity

Some of us already count hobbies as an essential part of our happiness; for others, hobbies feel more like a dream for another phase of life when you have less responsibility and fewer time constraints. Either way, hobbies deserve a slice of your pie.

Notice the difference between overly broad goals and achievable goals:

Broad: Make time for a hobby
Achievable: Carve out two hours a week for my hobby
Broad: Learn to surf
Achievable: Sign up for Sunday morning surfing lessons

The Pie Life

Here are some goals to consider for the hobbies slice:

- Schedule two hours for my hobby each week
- Join a sailing team
- Start a knitting circle
- Launch a baking club
- Take an improv class
- Incorporate my hobby into my life two days a week
- Organize a Saturday doubles tennis group
- Sell my creations on Etsy

As you can see, many of the above goals are tangible and achievable. When they are too broad, they become harder to tackle and we leave them behind. When we break down our goals into manageable steps, we are far more likely to achieve them. And the benefits don't just come from achievement; research shows that the mere pursuit of goals makes us more satisfied and happier with our lives.[10]

Goals Will Change

When TV anchor Gayle King was a young mom, her goal was to be in a top 10 market—meaning that of the 210 media markets in the United States, she would be a TV anchor in one of the top 10. Gayle's husband was at Yale Law School and she figured that they would take turns—she would ascend first in her career and then he would have his time later. Then maybe when the kids were 12 and 13, she would leave her career while his was taking the front seat.

But when the kids were 5 and 6, Gayle got divorced and all of that changed. As a single mom, she realized that she never wanted to give up her career and that she also liked the feel of Hartford, Connecticut, where she ultimately stayed for 18 years. She liked the community and enjoyed being a big fish in a small pond. And that is the thing about goals: they change over time because they need to adapt to your changing personal needs too. You never want to be so rigid that you can't adjust your goals to suit your life.

When Oprah Winfrey was thinking about giving up her show, she called her friend Gayle with a big opportunity. Oprah suggested that Gayle move with her two kids to Chicago to play a big role on *Oprah* and then, when it was time for Oprah to retire, Gayle would take over. It was a great succession plan for Oprah, and for Gayle it sounded like a dream job. But moving the kids to Chicago would mean taking them away from their dad and as Gayle explains, "At the end of the day that was not going to be good for them or good for him. I really wanted to do it, but their happiness and their connection and relationship to him was more important to me."

Gayle realized that at that moment, her kids' needs were more important than her career ambitions. And years later, she would get another huge opportunity when CBS called and asked her to co-anchor their morning show. Gayle calls the job "a dream I didn't even know I had!"

Now back to *your* dreams! Here is a worksheet to help you take your thinking further. You might want to adopt some of the sample goals above as your own, while others on the list might have sparked ideas for new goals.

Write your goals below:

Health:

_____

_____

_____

Career:

_____

_____

_____

Relationship:

_____

_____

_____

Children:

_____

_____

_____

Friends:

_____

_____

_____

Community:

_____

_____

_____

Hobbies:

_____

_____

_____

Putting your goals in writing is your first step toward making them an achievable reality. If they feel challenging, don't worry. Goals exist to push us; if they remain firmly in our comfort zone, it means that we are not striving for enough. Your goals are not only going to lead to practical life changes. They will also stretch you to get the most out of the life you lead. And you don't need to tackle them all at one time. Take a couple of slices and get cooking.

Now that you've identified your goals, in the chapters that follow we are going to explore the ingredients that will set you up for full success. Let's take a deep dive together into the conditions you need to achieve your optimal life and reach your full potential.

PART II

TOOLS

CHAPTER FOUR

THE PARTNERSHIFT

*I don't know of a single woman in a leadership position whose life
partner is not fully—and I mean fully—supportive of her career.*

— SHERYL SANDBERG

When I was 30, I remember sitting on the couch with friends in my apartment on West 85th Street in New York City and sharing our visions for the partners of our dreams. I had dreamed of finding someone who hadn't yet made it financially; I always thought a relationship would work better if we started out as equals, whereas if I met someone who had already built financial wealth and I hadn't, I might never feel like it was "ours." My romantic idea was that we would make it together. I was looking for someone ambitious yet grounded and kind but strong.

When I met Mitch, he fit the bill. Mitch was a hardworking entrepreneur who was putting blood, sweat, and tears into his latest company. We met on a blind date and after dinner and drinks, we walked uptown toward my home. Though I was wearing high heels, I was hoping that we could delay getting a cab for as long as possible. Neither of us mentioned the taxi and when we arrived at my building, we had walked 5.1 miles. It was love. We started out with no money, no kids, and no home. A life from scratch. What was our story going to be?

Our 100-guest wedding took place in Florida in January of 2005, only a few weeks after I had returned from a 23-city book tour that took me from Memphis to Seattle. By that time, my book, *The Experts' Guide to 100 Things Everyone Should Know How to Do*, had become a best seller and I was running a five-employee personal branding firm that represented luminaries from CEOs to chefs. My clients would call me at all hours of the night. One particular evening when I was lying in bed with my husband watching *The Bachelor*, a client called to say he had spotted a competitor of his in the pages of *Newsweek*. He demanded to know why my firm had never secured coverage for him in that magazine. As he spoke, I could practically see the steam coming from his ears; he was irate. I did my best to pacify him, but later, as I tried to fall asleep, I couldn't shake the feeling that this on-call, 24/7 lifestyle was unsustainable.

As fate would have it, my agent called a few months later telling me that Random House had offered me a three-book deal for the next books in my *Experts' Guide* series. I was driving through New England on a road trip with Mitch and we had stopped at a bead store. We were in the parking lot when I got the call and I was screaming and jumping up and down. Financially, the book deal was a hefty one that would finally allow us to buy our first apartment.

The place we found in Manhattan was only 900 square feet, but it was all ours. As I looked ahead at my life, I knew that I wanted to be a mom and that we wanted three children. In that moment, I decided that writing would be the perfect career for a new mom. I could do the books and parent and still contribute significantly to my family's bottom line. So I closed my firm and placed my employees in other companies. I shared the news with my clients and started to focus on making books and babies.

Only two years into this new plan, I ran into a problem. The books weren't challenging me enough. I wanted to be doing more. Yes, I found the books rewarding and time consuming for the six-month stretches when I was actually putting them together, but these periods were followed by six-month intervals when I had to wait for the books to be printed and published. I couldn't handle the lulls; I felt like I wasn't being productive enough. It was time to go in another direction and it was then that I met a guy named Gary Vaynerchuk, who convinced me to host an online talk show that he would produce. We called it *Obsessed TV* and set out to create the number one online talk show, like a Barbara Walters for the web. Almost overnight I had shifted gears, and the ripple effects were dramatic. Hosting the show on a full-time basis meant tweaking the division of labor with my husband and shaking up the system we had developed. No longer would I be spending more time with the kids during the "off season" of book publishing. We would have to figure out a new child-care schedule and a new routine for our relationship.

Other issues cropped up as well. By this point we had two children, Ella and Ruby, and Mitch's newly launched company had already exploded to 40 employees. He was coming home later and later and missing dinner, bath, and bedtime most nights. Left to handle the witching hours alone, I was becoming increasingly resentful. When Ella was an infant, we had implemented a "no TV" rule for the first two years, with one loophole: she could watch our wedding video and it wouldn't count. Now that I was doing the evening routine solo, I stuck her in front of the wedding video for an hour each night so I could take a break. When she began reciting the toasts by heart, I realized we had a problem. This was not how I had pictured our life, and it was far different than the vision Mitch and I had laid out together on our honeymoon. It was time for what I call a PartnerShift—a complete reconfiguration of our roles and how we managed our lives.

One night Mitch and I sat down together and I explained to him that I would rather give up the alone time we shared each night once the kids were asleep if it meant we could all eat dinner together and he could help with the bedtime routine. He was shaking his head before I could even finish my argument. "What message does it send to my employees if I leave the office by 5:30 each night? I can't possibly run the company and leave the office ahead of everyone else."

I pressed him on this. You see, when I was growing up, my own dad was not only home for dinner each night; he cooked the dinner too. My dad is a true Renaissance man. He was a success at work (he and my mom started and ran a small, six-person market research company), a wonderful chef at home, and a fantastic listener. He can sew a button that will survive the life of a shirt. Even today when I stay with my parents during trips to New York, my dad insists on ironing my dress so that it is wrinkle-free the next day for my presentation. His example is what led me to find a man who would be a partner to me in all aspects of life.

I turned to Mitch and insisted that we change the recipe. He agreed to sit down with the schedule, and we twisted and turned it like a Rubik's Cube. "What if you leave the office to get home for dinner at six each night and then go back to work at eight o'clock?" I suggested hopefully. To my surprise, he agreed to try it for a week. The next day Mitch asked his assistant, Dana, to start clearing his schedule after 5:30 each evening and to add calls to his calendar from 8:00 to 10:00 each night. It worked, but not without some challenges.

A few months into our new schedule, Mitch received a call from his most powerful investor. People think entrepreneurs are their own bosses and this is true—unless you have investors. When you have investors, you have many bosses. So this investor invited Mitch to his home—at night. He meant business.

He sat Mitch down and said, "We invest in entrepreneurs with cots in their offices, not entrepreneurs who leave at 5:30 each day." As Mitch tells it, after his initial shock and frustration wore off, he caught his breath and bravely said, "Well then, I will be the first entrepreneur to prove you wrong." And he did.

I am so proud of Mitch. He might not sew buttons, but he had the strength to stand up to an intimidating and powerful investor. And in doing so, he had sent a message to every woman and man in his company, showing them that male leaders need to make concessions to have a thriving personal *and* professional life.

I have always maintained that to reach your potential, you need to marry the right partner. And in case after case I have found this to be true. I remember hearing author Brené Brown speak at a conference and matter-of-factly state that when she wrote her last book, her husband "left town with the kids because I always go into this Jackson Pollock crazy thing where I am just writing in my researcher mode." You have to wonder what that time would have been like had Brené's husband *not* been there for her. He gave his wife the space to make her magic.

Every woman I've met who is reaching her potential is either single or has a true 50 percent partner. If you want your new pie to work, your partner is the essential first ingredient. Without an active and engaged teammate, your pie will crumble. I have yet to meet a successful, coupled woman who feels energized in her life but whose partner doesn't support her dreams by chipping in at home and beyond.

Living with an uninvolved or negative partner is far worse than having no partner at all. An unsupportive partner will deplete you of your energy, strength, and optimism. Conversely, closing the "domestic gap" leads to a happier union, because your resentment will give way to greater friendship and intimacy, which in turn makes your whole family happier. When was the last time you saw an unhappy kid with two happy, in love parents? Never! It hardly happens.

This chapter gives you the inspiration and the tactics to turn your existing relationship into one that enriches your life and helps propel you closer to your dreams. Any loving partner can implement a PartnerShift. When your partner feels a commitment to the team, he or she will be motivated to make it into the best partnership possible. As you will see, the change starts with you and the recipe is simple and easy to follow.

THE "WHO IS MY PARTNER?" QUIZ

Let's get a better understanding of who your partner is. This quiz applies to male/female partners because the same-sex couples I have worked with did not suffer from these kinds of issues.

1. You get a promotion at work. He:
    A. Surprises you with a reservation at your favorite restaurant to celebrate
    B. Tells you he is happy for you and goes back to reading the paper
    C. Is concerned that this will mean you are away from home more
    D. Tells you all the reasons why this is a disaster for your family life

2. After he goes to the bathroom, he:
    A. Puts the toilet seat down
    B. Usually puts the seat down and if he forgets, he is apologetic
    C. Can't seem to remember to put the seat down no matter how many times you tell him
    D. Asks, "Why should I put it down? Shouldn't you put it back up?"

3. You have a huge meeting tomorrow and you and your partner are both home for bedtime. He tells you he will put the kids to sleep so that you can work on your presentation. This scenario:
    A. Happens all the time
    B. Happens sometimes
    C. Could happen if I promised a massage or some other bribe
    D. Would happen only over his dead body

4. When with the kids, his relationship to his phone is:
    A. Nonexistent; he turns his ringer off
    B. Distant; he is rarely holding it
    C. Distracted; he checks frequently but not obsessively
    D. An appendage

Based on your answers, he will fall into one of four categories:

Mostly As: Great Guy. You picked well! Enjoy the ride!

Mostly Bs: Good at Heart Guy. You can do this!

Mostly Cs: 1950s Guy. A ton of work.

Mostly Ds: Unspeakable Guy. If he is an abuser or cheater, you must leave him.

What's Luck Got to Do With It?

If you haven't chosen your partner yet, good news: I can help you before you've made a poor choice. This sounds horribly negative, but the truth is that most women need to put much more thought into choosing their partners than they do.

Nothing drives me crazier than when women observe Mitch helping out with the kids and say to me, "What a great dad Mitch is! You're so lucky!" Yes, Mitch is a great dad. He deserves accolades, and I'm grateful to have him by my side. But luck had nothing to do with it. I knew what to look for, and it wasn't "tall, dark, and handsome," nor was it "successful and wildly ambitious." It was a kind-hearted, loving, open-minded, and ambitious man who knew how to make a commitment and stick to it.

Sounds simple, right? So here's my question: If we all know what Mr. Right looks like when we see him, why do so many of us marry Mr. Wrong? Because most women are not thinking far enough into their future when they fall in love. They are thinking about Mr. Right now instead of Mr. Right always. Many women have been raised to spend more time thinking about their weddings than thinking about their marriages. Questions like "What will I wear?" "What will the venue be?" and "What flowers will adorn the tables?" receive more attention than "Whose career will take precedence?" "How will we make decisions?" "How will we manage our finances?" "What kind of parents do we want to be?" and "How will we support each other's goals?" But at the end of the day, it is just the two of you. The wedding attendees are no longer there and you are in bed in sweatpants without makeup. Sure, you might have kids, but one day they will leave the house, launched into their own lives, and again it will be you and your partner alone. Who do you want by your side? Is it the affable guy who looks great in the photos, or the guy who will massage the crick in your neck when it hurts and take you out to celebrate your next promotion?

When Anne Fulenwider's kids were 1 and 3 years old, she began receiving a series of bigger and bigger jobs in magazine publishing. Then several years later she was offered a really big job—as editor in chief of *Marie Claire*. As Anne remembers, "I sat down with my husband and we had an honest conversation about whether or not we could handle all this. I almost didn't take the *Marie Claire* job because I wasn't sure what it would do to my family." Her husband pushed her to take the position, and he supports her by taking on "as much if not more responsibility for the kids' well-being as I do. It's something I was looking for in a husband. I wanted to build a family with someone who would be a very present father." There was no luck involved.

In a study of 25,000 Harvard Business School graduates,[11] it wasn't the women's lack of ambition holding them back; it was ending up in "traditional" marriages in which their husbands' careers were prioritized over theirs. At some point, many of these women took some time off and this further minimized their career opportunities, which made their careers take even more of a backseat. If they did end up leaving the workforce, it was typically as a last resort, not because of a lack of ambition or interest in working, but because their positions lacked fulfillment and offered little prospect of advancement.[12]

The New Mr. Right

If there was any luck involved in my choosing Mitch, it was that I was born into a family with parents who shared childrearing and a business together. My mom and dad ran our home and their company as equal partners. So I did have a head start in picking Mr. Right because I grew up with an amazing role model for a husband and father. If you didn't grow up with a role model like this, don't despair—I can capture Mr. Right for you in a simple checklist:

- Mr. Right supports your career and ambitions.

- He is proud of you when you achieve professionally.

- He doesn't expect to be waited on, but does expect to help.

- He loves children and isn't afraid to get silly, or dirty, playing with them.

- He makes plans in advance.

- He enjoys doing things for you, as you do for him.

- He knows who your friends are and makes an effort to connect with them.

- He chooses male friends who treat women respectfully.

- He doesn't feel competitive with you. Your wins are his too.

- He has your back. He sees the two of you as a team and is unflinchingly loyal.

So how did I meet my Mr. Right? I had asked friends, colleagues, and acquaintances to set me up with a man who was smart, kind, and confident. Can you tell which words are missing? "Good looking" and "rich." Neither of those is sure to last forever, but intelligence, a kind heart, and self-confidence sure do. (It was a bonus that Mitch turned out to be handsome and successful too!) I worked hard to meet my husband and, if you want to have the best life possible, you'll work hard to find yours too. Your future husband will not magically appear on your doorstep; you need to search for him with the right criteria in mind.

Dating is a volume game. If you were job interviewing, you would try to get your foot in the door with as many companies as possible to maximize your chances of finding the right fit. You would not feel good about going on only one job interview a month, so why settle for that ratio in your dating life? The more people you meet, the more likely you are to find one who is right for you.

When I met Mitch, online dating was not yet a big thing, so I worked the blind date circuit hard. I told everyone in my orbit, from friends to my hair stylist, that if they knew anyone great, to please set me up. I urged friends not to overthink it and showed my appreciation every time so that they would keep the matches coming. I never complained about the dates and kept it drama-free so that my friends and acquaintances would feel comfortable setting me up again. This meant I resisted telling friends about the date who didn't let the waiter put the bread basket down for fear it would devolve to him gaining back the 200 pounds he had just lost, or the guy who lost his car in the parking garage for 45 minutes and caused us to miss a movie, or the one who mistook biting for kissing. Seriously.

When single women today tell me they are looking for a relationship but won't go online, I don't believe they are really ready to meet someone. Opting out of online dating is like selling a great product but refusing to make it available to the world. Online dating is now the number one "distribution channel" for relationships, so how can you afford to close it off? Many women I've worked with have tried online dating but complain that they were inundated with all the wrong men as soon as they signed up. One way to combat this is to write your profile in the most confident way possible so as to weed out the insecure people. For example, writing "Education is very important to me" is far better than looking for someone with a big income. Stating how important education is to you is bound to weed out anyone who feels insecure about his intelligence. Use your profile as a filter; the more confident you sound, the more apt you are to attract the right suitors.

Finding Your Rhythm with Mr. Right

If you already have a husband, turning him into the supportive, sharing partner you need is somewhat trickier. Let's begin by reviewing what life looks like with Mr. Right by your side. The first thing to understand is that your experience at home won't ever be perfect. It's not about "perfect"—it's about finding someone who is willing to compromise and adjust (just as you are) so that you can get things done as a family while thriving as individuals. You also won't share the household chores equally at every moment. In fact, it is likely that you never will. A true partnership is one that breaks down 80:20 some days and 40:60 on others, or even 90:10 or 10:90 at times. Work ebbs and flows for both of you; sometimes you will be doing more than half the load at home, other times he will. If he has a big presentation or a surgery to perform the next day, you will step up. If you're on a business trip, it will be his turn.

Even in more typical weeks where there is no travel or pressing work obligation, splitting everything exactly in half is not always the best idea. Each of you should focus on what you do best and then pitch in to help each other as needed. Maybe you're a great cook and while you are busy in the kitchen, he loves to get on the floor and play Legos with the kids or sit down to a game of Uno. If you're more organized but can't stand waiting in line at the grocery store, perhaps he does the shopping every week and leaves it to you to pay the bills. Think about it: Would your company be doing well today if every employee did every job? Of course not. The same goes for your partnership.

Even with Mr. Right by your side, it can take time to fall into a rhythm. Mitch and I took a few years to figure out a morning routine that worked for our family. There were times when our arrangement seemed to be working but suddenly fell to pieces because the division of labor began weighing too heavily on one of us. Our routine is constantly shifting, but here is what works for us now: I am responsible for the upstairs. I gently wake the kids, get them dressed, and do their hair, while Mitch puts together their breakfasts and gets their lunches ready downstairs. Mitch also convinced me to outsource the grocery shopping to our nanny because I could benefit our family more by spending those two hours a week growing my business. So now our babysitter comes an hour early twice a week and does a grocery run; I've shown her the brands we like and the types of fruits and vegetables to buy.

Among the women I've worked with, I've come across a number of different partnership arrangements—it truly does run the gamut. As finance executive

Laura Flynn told me, her rhythm with partner Chris Pearlman "sort of happened naturally over the almost 10 years since our first son was born, and it was dictated by our different work schedules." When Chris isn't traveling, he handles all morning responsibilities until the sitter arrives at 7:45. Laura handles all evening responsibilities as well as any preparation required for the following morning. She packs the sports practice bags, fills water bottles, stacks clothes in the kitchen by activity, plans breakfast, and initials the homework. "That way, I know nothing gets lost in translation in the morning."

Olympic softball champion Jennie Finch and her husband, professional baseball player Casey Daigle, reside in Sulphur, Louisiana, where they are both hands on and involved in their three kids' daily lives. Jennie explains that for them, "it's less about dividing and conquering, and more about us doing as much as we can together."

Entrepreneur Kalika Yap and her husband Rodney manage their two careers and two daughters, ages 9 and 7, with a clear and deliberate division of labor. During the school year, Kalika drives the kids to and from school. During summer break, Rodney takes the kids to camp and she picks them up. As Kalika explains, "Rodney naturally falls into the role of being the primary parent when I am out of town or at a business event. I usually take the lead in their academics, selecting and signing up the kids for camps and enrichment like language, piano, and chess. Rodney takes the lead in sports like gymnastics, biking, soccer, and swimming. He does all the grocery shopping and cooks dinner often. He also is in charge of the household budget and bills, and plans our travel."

Alexandra Lebenthal, CEO of Wall Street's Lebenthal and Company, says of her husband Jay Diamond, "We've always had a very balanced relationship and I don't think I would have been as successful as a working mother without his contribution." What would she tell her own daughters? "Find a man who is truly going to be your partner." And to her son? "Be that man."

Now back to you! What kind of arrangement would you like to see with your partner? What tasks would each of you handle? Where is each of you at your best? As for the areas that neither of you like or are skilled at, how would you manage those? Is it possible to outsource any of them? What additional changes in your work or travel schedule could you and your partner make to run life together more effectively? Try mapping all of this out on a sheet of paper, placing your tasks on one side of the page and his on the other.

THE PLAY-TO-YOUR-STRENGTHS EXERCISE

What _____ does best   What _____ does best

_____   _____
_____   _____
_____   _____
_____   _____
_____   _____

Unclaimed activities

_____
_____
_____

Activity   Assigned to

_____   _____
_____   _____
_____   _____
_____   _____
_____   _____
_____   _____

Have fun with this exercise. Sit down and brainstorm the child-care and home activities that go into running your lives. Each of you takes what you do best and adds it to your column. Write down all unclaimed activities at the bottom of the page. When you're all done listing activities, divide these unclaimed activities in a way that seems fair and plays to your respective strengths.

Note: You don't want to get overly rigid with this; you need to roll with the punches a bit, but this is a great starting point.

The PartnerShift

Now that you've imagined what a more equitable household arrangement might look like, you face the task of getting your husband to buy in. Actually, that's not true: you might first face the task of getting *yourself* to buy in. On my radio show,

I fielded a call from Liza, a woman in St. Louis who was seeking advice on how to get more quality time for herself. When I asked Liza to describe her day, she relayed that she was a working mom of seven kids who ranged in age from 8 to 17. She woke up at the crack of dawn to go to work as a general manager of a car dealership. She was there all day, arriving home around six. All of her kids had a hand in preparing dinner together. They cooked, they ate, and after the kids went to sleep, Liza and her husband had sex every night (*not judging, but wowzers!*) at around eleven o'clock, at his insistence. She got four to five hours of sleep.

I asked Liza to tell me about her husband. What was *he* doing while she and the kids were preparing dinner? Her answer: he was sitting on the couch playing video games. In her world, that was okay—the man was the king of the castle, and the woman's job was to do the household chores, even if she worked. I asked Liza to consider what *exactly* her husband was bringing to the relationship. She couldn't come up with anything. Aside from working part-time, her husband was total deadweight. She worked to support him as well as their seven kids, but unlike the kids, he did not help out at all with the chores necessary to making the home run smoothly. He was getting a free ride, and it came at the expense of all the "me time" Liza needed and craved.

As bad as it sounds, the blame didn't just rest squarely on her husband's shoulders. Liza shared some fault for this less-than-ideal situation too. Even as we spoke, she had a hard time acknowledging her husband's failure as a partner; her traditional beliefs about male and female roles were too ingrained. Finally I asked her, "What will you say if your daughter brings home a man just like your husband?" She gasped and said she hoped that would never happen but if it did, she would tell her to dump him immediately. Only then did a light bulb go off in Liza's head about her own life.

If you're like Liza, struggling with a deadweight partner but believing that it's "natural" or "normal" for a woman to do most of the work, it's time to get real. It obviously makes *no sense* that women are now 50 percent of the work-force but still do more than 70 percent of the work at home.[13] When you are working hard and momming hard and wifing hard all on your own, you will not maintain any semblance of sanity. You can't do all the laundry, all the house-work, all the doctors' appointments, all the shopping, and all the cooking *and* still function as a happy, well-adjusted human being. If you want to have a suc-cessful career and be a loving partner, a great mom, and a healthy person, you need to get rid of the traditional beliefs that might be holding you back.

Once you do that, you're ready to embark on a PartnerShift. A PartnerShift entails a complete reworking of how you and your partner organize your daily lives and how you both organize your life together. It requires a dramatic shift of behavior—and attitude—from both of you. If your partner has been doing 10 percent of the work at home and you have been doing 90 percent, then that says something about *both* of you, because you have enabled that ratio just as much as he has. *Expect* him to be a partner, but help him to be one too.

Starting From Scratch

Let's look at the things you can do to bring about a PartnerShift . . .

First: Stop making excuses for your partner. Pre-PartnerShift moms love to tell me how busy their men are. These men are supposedly "needed for a deal" all the time or they "have bosses who would never tolerate an early departure" from work or they "are under intense pressure to meet deadlines and financial milestones." Stop making excuses. No matter how much pressure your partner faces, he could still do more at home.

If I wanted to, I could have made any number of excuses for my husband. His company was growing rapidly. He had seven investors breathing down his neck, their money and reputations on the line. He had employees whose livelihoods depended on him. He had a young, growing family whose financial security was at risk if his new company failed. But as the old saying goes, if there is a need, there is a way to meet it, and Mitch has indeed come through as a partner with flying colors. Your husband can too.

Second: Be willing to part with your old-fashioned domains. Women tend to declare that their jobs at home are too complicated for anyone to take over. From picking out the right food at the grocery store to doing the laundry the *right* way to packing lunchboxes, we take pride in thinking that we simply cannot be replaced. Of course we can. If you've ever had a C-section, been acutely sick, or taken an overnight business trip, you know that your partner is perfectly capable of keeping the home going without you—even if it's not exactly how you'd do it. So should he pitch in only when an emergency strikes? Stop treating men like babies. You already entrust them with your plants, your pets, even your physical and mental well-being. So why do you believe that they can't shoulder more in the home?

What you expect your husband to do will of course vary depending on your kids' ages and developmental stages. Here is a checklist that covers some of the biggies, as well as some suggestions for how to make it easier for him to participate:

Pregnancy

✓ *Doctors' appointments.* From conception to birth, there are a seemingly endless array of checkups and tests over the nine months of pregnancy. Add them to his calendar and make sure he is there to see the ultrasound image with you. Your partnering pattern starts now!

✓ *Prenatal classes.* You take these classes together. Period.

✓ *Preparation.* Read pregnancy books together—even just a page a night! Have him help decorate the nursery and choose baby gear (strollers, car seats, etc.).

✓ *Parental leave.* How much time can each of you spend at home? Will you take your parental leave together or stagger it for maximum coverage? The time to talk child care is *before* the baby arrives.

Infant/Toddler/Preschool

✓ *Parental duties.* Bathing, dressing, feeding, reading stories, playing, and nighttime wakings—these are all jobs for *both* of you.

✓ *Doctor's appointments.* Attend pediatrician wellness visits together, or take turns doing so. Come up with a general (but flexible) system beforehand to determine which of you will leave work to tend to a sick child.

✓ *Day care.* Have him get to know the staff at day care. If you will be hiring a nanny, he needs to be involved with researching, interviewing, and choosing the final candidate.

✓ *Activities or preschool.* Get your partner involved in deciding which activities will fill your children's days, such as music classes or sports. This includes picking out the right preschool. These are family decisions, not mom decisions.

✓ *Milestones.* All of the milestones that require parental involvement, such as the transition to solid foods and potty training, should be discussed and handled by both of you.

✓ *Familiarity.* Have your partner get to know the teachers and your child's schedule, as well as the bus or carpool routine. Attend parent-teacher conferences together.

✓ *Schoolwork.* Have your partner help with homework. Be smart about it—if you're the math whiz and he's the history buff, divvy up the homework help accordingly.

✓ *Activities.* Engage your partner in planning birthday parties, playdates, and weekend outings.

I always encourage new moms to find excuses to leave their partners alone with a new baby within the first few days. If you don't, Dad will never gain the confidence necessary to step in proactively next time. Remember, much of what you do, from picking out your kids' clothing to changing diapers, is something your partner could do too.

Try this: When you need your partner to take over a new task, treat him as an employee replacing a fellow worker. He can shadow you to learn every aspect of the day that he hasn't already overseen. He can take pictures of you assembling the kids' lunchboxes, he can watch as you wake them or comfort them and do bath time—everything can be learned.

Third: Give your husband space to learn what to do, especially when it comes to parenting. I am often asked to counsel couples when they're struggling to parent their first child, and it's typically the wife who has initiated contact. She assumes that I will tell her husband all the ways he is failing as a spouse and father, but many times, if there is fault, it's with the mom. Without even realizing it, she has written off her spouse as an incompetent buffoon and micromanages his every interaction with the child. Understandably, this demotivates him to get involved, and he distances himself more and more from caring for the baby. Coupled with her low expectations, this makes for a very bad start to the parenting partnership.

If your boss was constantly hovering over you, telling you that everything you were doing was wrong, how would you feel? Would you still feel inspired to come to work every day, or would you begin to dread work and doubt your own abilities? This is what happens when you micromanage your partner *with his own child.* A good rule of thumb: if the baby is not in danger, bite your tongue. After I spoke to a group of moms recently, one new mom of a 10-month-old approached me and said, "I am so overwhelmed and exhausted and I never let my husband help." I asked her what would happen if she left her husband alone with her baby. "He would do things differently than I would," she said. Almost instantly, after hearing herself verbalize this, something clicked. "I need to get over it."

All of us—partners included—tend to rise to the expectations set for us. Just as it would never occur to me that my husband would be anything less than a 50 percent partner, it should never occur to you that yours would be, either. You don't want to be the woman who says, "My husband would *never* change a diaper." Instead, be the woman who says, "Honey, I'm cooking dinner. Could you go upstairs and change Emmet?" or, "I'd like to go out for a 30-minute run. Could you put Chloe down for her nap?" Gradually get him more involved by transforming your expectations and incorporating him into the daily culture of your home. You'll be amazed by what happens.

One Sunday, some close friends came over for dinner. My friend was marveling at my husband's hosting skills, telling me that her husband would never be that helpful. Minutes later her husband had to leave to pick up his mom at the doctor. "Do you want me to stop at the supermarket and get you anything on the way home?" he asked. What happened next was the turning point, the moment when this man became transformed from the "unhelpful" husband she described into the "unable to help" husband she was helping to create. My friend responded, "You wouldn't know what to get. Don't worry about it." Ouch. In that moment, my friend blew her opportunity to get her husband more involved. Even worse, she discouraged him from trying to help in the future.

Fourth: Support your partner as he begins to tackle new tasks. It's important to praise more than criticize. Catch him doing things right. "I love how you dressed Caleb." "What a great idea to sign Leila up for swim classes." "Look how Mateo is responding to you as you feed him. He ate the avocado for the first time." Lay off the criticism and pile on the accolades. A diaper put on backwards never hurt anyone. A mismatched outfit, an unhealthy dinner every once in a while—these things are not important. Having your partner step up to the plate is important.

One Saturday, Susan came home after lunch with a friend to find her husband and 2-year-old daughter having a dance party during what was supposed to be the child's nap time. She got upset with her husband, they argued, and she said, "Thanks for nothing! I can't even be out with my friend." She didn't give him a chance to explain that he had tried to get her down for an hour, finally gave up, and started playing with her. Susan regretted her reaction and realized that even if nap time was blown, it had been replaced by bonding time and fun. A missed nap and a dance party are the makings of a great memory.

Fifth: Communicate, communicate, communicate. Or as I like to say, maintain a constant "partnersation." We all know that a successful relationship requires constant communication. Daily, weekly, nightly. It is impossible to overcommunicate (especially with kids in the mix), because there simply isn't enough time in the day to get everything done. So your PartnerShift requires a big conversation to get things going, and many more conversations to keep your husband and you on track.

Do your home a favor and *start today*. You will come up with a million excuses why you should wait a week or a month before broaching the PartnerShift. It's his birthday. It's your daughter's first day of school. He is in the middle of a big negotiation. You are leaving for a family trip. All of that may be true, but there is never an ideal time to have a tough conversation. If you wait a month, you'll wish you had started a month ago. There is nothing stopping you from making these small yet doable changes *today*. You can do it! You are strong and committed to making your relationship and family function as smoothly as possible. You know what you need!

How do you handle that first conversation? One way is simply to take the direct route and say, "I am unhappy and exhausted, and we don't have enough alone time together." Use "I" statements instead of "you"—it shifts the conversation from placing blame on him ("You aren't doing enough around here!") to addressing your legitimate needs. Use "you" only when you are saying positive, proactive things like, "You can help me. We need to be more of a team." When you put him on the defensive, he will continue to defend himself. Put him in the role of the future hero instead. Remember, it's all about setting high expectations.

Begin by taking out two sheets of paper. Each of you should write down all of the things you are already doing: planning playdates, putting a child to sleep, managing the sitter, filling out forms, paying the bills, buying the kids' shoes, planning birthday parties. Everything you and your partner do, big and small, should be added to these lists. When couples compile lists like these, they end up surprised. Keep an open mind. Your partner might be doing more than you realized, or he might be aghast at how much you are doing. Simply listing activities like this is often enough to transform your life together moving forward. If you have chosen a rational man as your partner, he will be moved to fix a situation that looks incredibly lopsided. This is your time to redistribute the division of labor. It might take a few fits and starts; it might require that you and your partner go back to square one and swap some of the duties that play more to your respective strengths. Eventually, with your shared commitment to getting it right, a new, more manageable routine will take shape.

To keep this new routine running smoothly, make a ritual of going over the weekly or daily schedule together. As I've said, a "50/50 home" doesn't mean you are each doing identical work, but rather that you are dividing and conquering. You can only do that if you are on the same page about who is in charge of dinner each night, who is doing drop-offs and pick-ups, who is scheduling doctors' appointments, and so on. If one or both of you travel for work, the earlier you know your partner's schedule, the easier it will be to plan and run your life. Conflicts will arise and you will be *constantly* negotiating, but if you're like me, you'll find that just reviewing your schedules together out loud will make it all seem more doable.

Taking the Entrepreneurial Approach

Don't take a PartnerShift lightly. This isn't just some little exercise you are going to try on like a pair of shoes at Macy's. This is a new phase of your marriage—a reboot, or better yet, a start-up. You need to treat it like any venture you might launch. Put in the commitment required to get this "business" off the ground.

Like any start-up, your PartnerShift will have its share of growing pains. Stick with it. Celebrate the accomplishments. And be sure to nurture your marriage as well. It shouldn't *all* be work, and it shouldn't *all* be about the kids. Romance counts. Some of the most depressed women I know have thrown themselves wholeheartedly into their kids' lives and woken up years later to find their kids ready to move out of the house, leaving them home alone with a partner they barely know. The healthiest marriages are those where the parents are actively connected with each other—mentally, physically, and emotionally.

THE EARNINGS GAP EXCUSE

What happens when the primary breadwinner uses making more money as an excuse for doing far less or none of the child care and housework? If your partner confronts you with an argument like this, don't buy into it. When a woman leaves the workforce completely, she will likely have a hard time getting back in, and even if she does, she will likely never reach her full financial potential. Even if you are the sub-earner (the lesser-earning partner), you still need to maintain your career in the event that something unexpected happens to your partner. So keeping your network warm and your skills sharp is essential to your family's financial safety. To help you maximize your career and earning potential, there needs to be a more equal division of labor at home.

Consider too the health and happiness of your kids. When he is doing his share at home, the noneconomic returns for you (job satisfaction, personal fulfillment, confidence) have a tangible effect on daily household happiness. And kids are so much more successful when both parents stay involved in their care. Research shows that absentee fathers are the single greatest risk factor in teen pregnancy for girls.[14] And girls who see their fathers contributing at home are less likely to end up in traditional marriages (defined as a breadwinning dad who doesn't help at home and a stay-at-home mom who cleans and takes care of the kids).[15]

The time to launch your start-up (or, if you're single, to start seeking out Mr. Right) is *now*. If you want a satisfying career, a happy home, and a solid marriage, you need a partner who "gets it" and is willing to work side by side with you. It begins with your partner—and with you. Young kids are only young kids once. You can never re-create this time with them. Their childhoods and views of the world are being shaped *as you read this book*, so the changes you need to make to your life cannot possibly happen soon enough. Sit down with your partner tonight and start looking at your schedules. How can you spend more time together as a family? How can you manage your life better as a team? You want to lead a fulfilling life, but you can't have a delicious pie without him doing his share of work. If you are drowning in a workload that is consistently uneven, your recipe will never taste quite right. But if you can readjust the ingredients, you will be one giant step closer to baking the delicious pie that is your new life.

CHAPTER FIVE

YOU AT WORK

I didn't get there by wishing for it or hoping for it, but by working for it.

— ESTÉE LAUDER

There might be no busier person on the planet right now than television show creator Shonda Rhimes. Shonda has three shows on TV and three daughters at home. Her e-mail signature offers a peek into what makes her successful in managing both roles, television executive and mom. It reads:

Please Note: I will not engage in work e-mails after 7 pm or on weekends.
IF I AM YOUR BOSS, MAY I SUGGEST: PUT DOWN YOUR PHONE.

When I asked Shonda what inspired the signature, she explained that because of e-mail, everyone works 24 hours a day now. She tried not answering e-mails in the evenings but that just resulted in a litany of hysterical-sounding follow-ups; people couldn't cope with the lack of response. Her solution: "I decided to train everyone. I made it my e-mail signature, so that every single time someone got an e-mail from me, they were also reading that I wasn't going to answer them if they e-mailed me after 7:00 p.m." But then Shonda realized that although she was happier, the people who worked for her still felt required to e-mail, whether or not she was responding. So she added the "suggestion" to her signature, which is really just a note giving them permission to turn off their phones and enjoy their families and their lives without guilt. Shonda explains, "I believe it makes a fundamental difference in the quality of our evenings and weekends to know that we aren't expected to be 'on' if we don't want to be."

What can you do if your boss is not as wonderful as Shonda? How do you assert healthy boundaries at work without getting fired or feeling like the hammer will drop? Tracy, an accountant at one of the biggest accounting firms in the country, wasn't happy with her work life. Every day she would try to sneak out of her office around 5:30 p.m. so she could make it home by 6:30 to see her kids. Still, at least three nights a week, she found herself chained to her desk by a late-day request or a last-minute conference call. Each afternoon, Tracy became extremely anxious about her daily departure hours before she was set to leave. Once 4:00 p.m. hit, she literally hid behind her desk, worrying that if she looked a colleague in the eye for too long, she would be pulled into a late-afternoon meeting or asked for help with a new project.

At home, it was no better. Because Tracy intended to arrive home at 6:30, her nanny worked from 8:00 in the morning until 6:30 every day. Most nights, Tracy had to make the "call of shame" to her nanny, apologizing for being delayed at work yet again. Her nanny became frustrated with her own unpredictable work hours, and Tracy found herself worrying whether her nanny might be taking out her frustration on the kids. As Tracy's children got a bit older, they began to call and ask her when she would be coming home, and when she called announcing she'd be late, her son would grab the phone out of the nanny's hand and shower Tracy with a guilt trip. Her son often burst into tears during these calls, and when Tracy hung up, she cried too.

What could Tracy do to end this downward spiral of discontent and guilt? We came up with a six-part plan:

1. *Decide what's really important.* Tracy's first step was to pin down her nonnegotiables. She decided that she wanted to be home by 6:30 every evening, and she wanted two hours of uninterrupted time with her kids every weeknight before they went to bed.

2. *Stop sneaking out.* Tracy was leaving the office hoping colleagues wouldn't notice, but it wasn't working for her and it was probably far more obvious than she realized. So from here on out, Tracy would start addressing her work schedule head-on. The next day she went into her manager's office and announced a new plan to her boss: "I'd like to have a more predictable schedule. I will aim to leave work at 5:30 every day and I will stay late if there is a work emergency or deadline to meet. I will be back online after 8:30 once my kids are asleep." Without an ounce of hesitation, her boss obliged. This might not happen every time, but there is always a good chance that it will. And if your boss says no, you have at least stepped up and fought for what you need. You now know what you are dealing with, and you can make a decision from there.

3. *Train your colleagues.* To set expectations, Tracy started spreading the word about her new schedule. Her colleagues didn't push back overtly; their resistance showed itself in other ways. Coworkers continued to schedule 5:00 p.m. meetings that she needed to be part of, or they would throw new work on her desk at the end of the day. When this happened, Tracy calmly explained that she could participate in meetings between 8:30 a.m. and 5:00 p.m., unless there was an emergency. Each time a colleague would venture outside of her time boundaries, she would again patiently explain her new schedule. Over the course of six months, Tracy's colleagues stopped asking for the late-day meetings. She had trained them to respect her boundaries, and she had dropped her own guilt about leaving.

4. *Set boundaries at home.* This is a big one. Tracy committed to being home by 6:30 p.m. and to turning her technology back on at 8:30. Sometimes her kids would get out of bed after she had put them to sleep when she was trying to work. She handled this by saying, "This is Mommy's work time and your sleep time." Eventually, her kids began to respect her boundaries. When they didn't, her husband stepped in to take over so that she could catch up on her work.

5. *Announce a work emergency plan.* Tracy told her colleagues that she would be back on e-mail at 8:30 after her kids went to sleep but that if they needed her urgently between 6:30 and 8:30, they could call her home phone. This happened only once in the year after she stopped sneaking around. Just having this backup plan in place made her colleagues and boss feel more comfortable about her two "unreachable" hours.

6. *Let go of the guilt.* Tracy learned to compartmentalize, and she didn't feel guilty about it. She didn't buy into those images we see of the mom in a business suit holding a baby, a laptop, and a phone, working and parenting at the same time. When she was at work, she focused on being awesome at work. When she was home, she felt great about turning off the smartphone and being present for her family. Of course she experienced a tiny sense of dread when she turned her phone on at 8:30 to see what she had missed, but it was almost always something minor and this left Tracy even more confident

that the boundaries she had set were the right ones. Whenever guilt threatened to creep back in during times when she had to work a little more, Tracy remembered that the best thing she could do for her family was to be her best self while "on the clock," whether she was at the office, on a business trip, or handling e-mails after the kids were in bed. When you are giving your all to work, you are more successful, you gain job security, and you feel good about your output, benefitting your family financially and emotionally.

Tracy wasn't working less, she was working smarter, and she had designed a schedule that met her family's needs without sacrificing her performance. She was no longer sneaking around the office or feeling tremendous guilt at home the way she had when she was checking e-mail all the time and feeling only half present. Tracy felt significantly less stress at work once she had acclimated her colleagues to her new schedule, and this meant that she could protect her time with the kids at night.

Emily Woodward didn't have that sense of calm. "This is it," Emily thought. "I will almost certainly be fired." A blizzard was sweeping across Boston, and school had been unexpectedly canceled. Her kids were home, and since Emily had nobody to care for them, she would be home too. She e-mailed her colleagues to tell them that she would be working from home but available by phone or e-mail all day. Emily planned to use a combination of naps, screen time, and a liberal use of the mute button when she would be on calls.

As she pressed "send," she could barely breathe, anticipating her colleagues' reactions. They would think she wasn't taking her job seriously, and that she was unreliable. If they didn't fire her, they would certainly pass her up for a promotion, writing her off as "just a mom."

What came next shocked Emily: her colleagues didn't blink an eye. They accepted her absence and moved on, business as usual. Looking back on it now, she says, "When you make it seem normal to focus on deliverables instead of face time, it can become so." Since being at home that day wasn't impeding her workflow, and since Emily had delivered, her colleagues had followed her lead. One of her staff members subsequently told Emily that she felt she was more available and responsive to her that day—due to a combination of Emily overcompensating for her absence and not running from meeting to meeting as she typically did when in the office.

One of the most confusing parts of being a working parent is figuring out where your life ends and your work begins. How will you navigate a flexible schedule? Or business travel? How will you handle it when unexpected crises pop up at work? On the other hand, how will you bring life to work without overdoing it? Will you wallpaper your office with photos of your kids? Will you pretend you don't have a child home sick from school or that your son's play is not on the same day as the corporate retreat? Will you let guilt trips from your family get you down? Unless you have a strategy for managing work and life, such issues will linger and worsen, much like a recurring cold becomes a chronic illness. You'll never transcend your existing life to achieve a new, more exciting, more energizing life. So, let's take a moment to think through the relationship between your work and your life. Let's make a plan for how you will bake up a life that works.

Defining Your Nonnegotiables

When we switched my daughters to a new school, it was during "odd" years (as opposed to more typical kindergarten or seventh-grade entry points) so the adjustment was more difficult for them. Ruby and Ella were each one of only two new kids joining their grades. To ease the transition, when it came time to volunteer to help out at the school, I signed us up to be end-of-year party hosts, something we had done for my son's preschool each year. I figured it would make my third-grader happy when I told her at breakfast the next morning. And it did.

When the following June came around, there was a problem. I had been asked to speak at Alt Summit, a design conference I had always wanted to be part of. In my giddy excitement I had said yes before checking the calendar. When I did finally look, I realized that the conference took place on what was to be the girls' last day of school *and* the day of the end-of-year party.

I worked some magic to move the party one day earlier, but I still had to miss the last day of school because of my commitment to the conference. I didn't know if my kids would remember, but I knew that I would. This episode launched a new rule in our home. Just like birthdays, the first and last days of school are blackout days. Unless completely necessary, we won't miss them.

Other women I know make similar rules for themselves and their families. For maternity wear designer and single mom Liz Lange, Friday night dinners are untouchable; Liz and her teenage kids simply do not make plans on Friday nights. "That is a night where we have dinner together with our extended family.

If somehow we have lost touch with one another a bit during the week, we know we are all coming together on Friday nights."

It pays to figure out what your nonnegotiables are. Once you do, you can set boundaries to protect them. Do you need to make sure nobody touches your Sundays? Do you need to be at every one of your daughter's softball games or never miss a pediatrician appointment? Deciding on your nonnegotiables means reconciling what you want and what is practical, given your lifestyle.

Perhaps you really enjoy having family breakfasts every day but you are a teacher and need to be in the classroom too early to make that happen. Or you might want to be at every soccer game but realize that fall is your busy season at work and making it to 14 soccer games would jeopardize your results. There are some things you will need to give up. Whatever the case, setting a few clear, nonnegotiable boundaries between work and life is a key ingredient in any woman's delicious pie. Be realistic—but be strong.

Times Are a Changing and You Will Too!

A generation ago, when most people worked from nine to five and before we had technology that allowed us to work remotely, a church/state separation existed between work and home. Now we live in the era of gyms, dry cleaning, and your favorite foods—at work! Employers have created environments that cater to *living at work*. As millennials have taken the spotlight, companies are competing to win their loyalty. Ping-pong and pool tables at the office emotionally connect younger workers to their companies, but they can spell disaster for a working parent who has places to go and little people to see—at home. At the same time, we now have devices that allow us to stay connected long after we have left the office. This provides the flexibility to go to your son's baseball game without being completely out of touch.

In companies that encourage you to spend more time at the office, leaving early or arriving late can draw far more attention than it would in a work culture with clearer boundaries. If you have to run out to your daughter's lacrosse game, or you need to stay home to take your sick child to the doctor, your boss and colleagues are going to notice. So, what to do?

Many women feel powerless against the pressure created by employers to merge work with life. But if you are doing good work, you are far from powerless. You just have to step up and claim the work/life boundaries you want, so that work nourishes your life rather than detracts from it. As Kristal Bergfield, head of customer service at a technology company, notes, "The work/life balance is *my* responsibility to manage, not my employer's. If I feel that I've been working too much and am feeling burned out or disconnected from my family, especially after a business trip or a hectic product launch, I take a personal day or make sure that I take my kids to school or cook dinner."

TV meteorologist Audrey Puente credits close attention to boundaries with getting her through the busy days of momming and working. "When I am with my children, I do not answer my phone to chat with friends. When I am with my friends, I call the kids before I walk into the restaurant so I can focus while at dinner. When I am at work, I schedule myself time to call the kids, answer e-mails, and update social media. When I am asleep, I shut my phone off. I feel that if I focus 100 percent at the current task, I can then move on to take care of the next task and everything gets covered."

Keep Your Home Life Where It Belongs—At Home!

Once you've established boundaries for yourself, you can't get complacent. You have to reinforce those boundaries day in and day out by *being extremely careful not to bring your life to work*. So many of us bring our life to work without even realizing it. We take conference calls from home with our kids jetting in and out of the room. We go on vacation and send photos of our feet in a beach chair to our boss. We go on a little too long in meetings about our kids' gymnastics feats. If we really want our colleagues to respect our family time, we need to make it extremely clear that we respect our work time too.

At a few organizations, strict boundaries are part of the culture, and it really helps. If you walk down the halls of Fox News, you'll be struck by the sea of smiling faces. The world could be blowing up or there could be a torrential downpour outside but for some reason, the employees of Fox News are still smiling, from the makeup artists to the news directors. Regardless of your politics, you want a sip of whatever Kool-Aid they have been drinking.

I once had the chance to ask Roger Ailes, president of Fox News, how he hires his employees. His answer has stuck with me ever since: "I hire people who when asked how they are, never tell the truth." I love this response because when you are at work and you pass someone in the hall exchanging "Hi! How are you?" niceties, you really don't have time to process any answer but "Great!" It's even worse with the coworkers you sit with; when they start talking about their car payments or the fight they had with their mother-in-law, they have suddenly shaken the work boundaries and brought the whole group down with them. The next time you see the colleague with the big issue, you feel compelled to ask a follow-up question to see how she is doing. You have entered into a relationship at work that conflicts with your own desire to be efficient, effective, and professional.

Save the car payment talk and the issue at school for your best friend, your spouse, or your mom. If you share the gory details of your life with your colleagues, they will share too, and you will all watch lost minutes turn into lost hours. Meanwhile, the more intimate your relationships with colleagues, the more you risk getting involved in office politics.

This doesn't mean you want to be the office outcast. Chime in about the latest episode of *Homeland*, and when the guy in accounts payable complains about the lines he encountered at Disneyland over the weekend, feel free to share your story too. We all need work friends, and you will be far happier if you have one or two that you can count on. But choose your friends wisely and patiently. A great work friend is a well-liked colleague with a positive attitude, more apt to cheerlead than to gossip, a loyal person whom you enjoy being around and talking to. But once you have that friend, there is no need to broadcast the friendship over a loudspeaker. Take the relationship outside of the office so that it can really blossom.

Choose Your Work Situation Wisely

I've focused on how we can reshape our own mindsets to stay strong about our boundaries, but there's also an external dimension to address. Your work environment and habits you choose for yourself matter. The right environment will make it relatively easy to stick to your boundaries and feel good about your role. Pick the wrong one and you're positioning yourself for needless conflict and angst.

Not all employers are created equal—especially for working parents. Here are some important factors to consider:

1. *Parental leave policies.* Though the United States lags behind every other developed country in our parental leave policies, American companies that offer paid leave are becoming more common. The best company is the one that offers paid maternity *and* paternity

leave. This implies that the company is treating moms and dads as equals, in turn suggesting that the company will show less bias against promoting and hiring moms going forward. There has been a recent shift in these policies; as of this book's publication date, companies like Netflix are leading the way with unlimited leave for up to a year. Technology company Adobe offers up to 16 weeks. Facebook, Bank of America, Google, Goldman Sachs, Twitter, and Microsoft have also adopted generous policies.

2. *The absence of a "live your life at work" culture.* The company with the gym, the restaurant, and the dry cleaner—all at the office? Chances are you won't hear the wind howling there when 6:00 p.m. comes around; you'll hear lots of typing and people working the phones. Leave that for others. Instead, choose a company where making it home for dinner doesn't make you the anomaly.

3. *Your ability to see an "older you" at the company.* When you go to a job interview, do you see women that are like you but 10 or even 20 years older? If so, that is a good sign. Being the workplace pioneer is exhausting and challenging—probably the last thing you need as a busy working mom. As Lisa Miller so eloquently explained in a 2015 essay for *New York* magazine, "The better plan would be for a young woman to enter a workplace and, upon looking around, see lots and lots and lots of established, successful females from which to collate a vision of herself: the loner, the sycophant, the ass-kicker, the honest broker, the backstabber, the flirt, the wheedler, the warm hug, the cold fish, the brainiac, the yeller, the whisperer, the diplomat, the hoop-jumper, the straight-A student, the zealot, the do-gooder. Role models don't have to be superheroes, in other words, or even necessarily exemplary; there just have to be enough of them, and they have to have made it work."[16]

4. *Fluid communication.* Fear-based leadership runs rampant in companies. In workplaces where it does, everyone walks on eggshells and employee concerns remain buried deep under the surface. For you to reach your potential at work, you need an environment with fluid communication between managers and colleagues. Most job

interviews end with, "Do you have any questions for me?" This is a great opportunity to get a better sense of the culture. Feel free to ask how issues are handled in the organization. What is communication like? You can also do your research by talking to other employees about their experiences.

The Flextime Fantasy

Imagine, at the extreme, that you enjoy a totally flexible schedule. On Monday morning you are running out the door with your daughter, and your husband calls after you, "Would you mind picking up my shirts at the dry cleaner?" You say yes. When you arrive at school you run into Tammy, who invites you to coffee with a few of the other moms. You agree to meet them at the coffee shop down the street once you finish dropping off your daughter. When you go to your child's classroom you see the teacher, who tells you that another parent just dropped out of Thursday's field trip. Could you chaperone the trip instead? You agree to do it. On the way to the coffee shop, you listen to voicemail and hear your sister asking if you wouldn't mind picking up the birthday gift for your mom because she has to be at the office and her boss is watching her like a hawk. In the course of just one hour, you have lost seven hours of work time because of your flexible schedule. It is wonderful that you have the opportunity to say yes to all of these compelling things, but doing so without limits comes with a price.

As a working parent, you need to change your idea of flextime. Managing a flexible schedule well doesn't mean always putting work after play; it means that you will now use your flexibility to intentionally choose your work hours. So whereas your friends without a flexible schedule need to clock in and out of the office at times dictated by someone else, you can decide when those times will be. But here's the point: you still have times for clocking in and out. A flexible schedule does *not* mean no schedule.

Set clear and strict rules for yourself. I know an author who decided that she would write every day from ten in the morning to two in the afternoon. This made it easy for her to turn down lunch dates and avoid scheduling doctors' appointments during her designated work time. She treated her work time as unchangeable, guaranteeing herself 20 hours of writing time each week. If you have a flexible job, you need to set your schedule too.

Betty, an empty nester from Ohio, called in to my radio show to talk about the challenges of her "flexible" schedule. She ran her own business and the work-flow fluctuated, but lately she felt like she wasn't being efficient and was constantly feeling guilty about letting her friends and family down. When pressed, Betty explained that because she worked for herself and from home, her elderly mother, neighbors, and friends constantly dropped by, taking offense when she told them she had to work. Working fixed hours each day would not suffice because her schedule was fairly unpredictable. One day she might have 10 hours of work, the next day 3. What to do?

The one predictably available part of Betty's day was her nights, so we used those and decided that she would proactively set a weekly dinner date with her mom. On another night, she would invite her neighbors for weekly cocktails. The prospect of this delighted Betty, and she knew that her friends and her mom would be excited by this weekly plan as well. She set boundaries in her personal life, and these led to greater success at work.

This does not mean you need to be a type A stickler about your schedule at all times. Part of the reason you wanted to have the flexible schedule is so you could say yes—but do so smartly. If you say yes to everything, you will lose all control over your schedule and in no time you will be borrowing from Suzy to pay Dave. In your case, when you say yes to everything, you end up cheating your career slice and then you might need to steal from your kids slice or relationship slice or friends slice to make up for it—and this might force you to say no to something you really wanted to do. So when working flexibly, use your management muscle to set at least some boundaries for yourself.

Managing the Business Trip

When TV host and former Olympic medalist Summer Sanders travels for work, she is all business. She says, "It is all about maximizing my time away from home. When I plan my work trips, I make sure every moment is productive." So do I. By packing in as many meetings and meals as possible, I make my travel virtually guilt-free (even without reciting my mantra!), I fulfill my obligations, and then I fill in any gaps by meeting new contacts or networking.

Before I left on a whirlwind tour to speak at women's conferences in Texas, Massachusetts, and Pennsylvania, I looked at the roster of other speakers and gathered together a small group for dinner on the night before each event. Some of the women I invited were preexisting contacts, while other invitations were extended via cold e-mails I sent introducing myself. By the time the conferences began, I already felt like I had been productive just by having had the chance to bond with successful women from all over the country. Making business trips as full as possible eliminates the guilt, and if you can get a good night's sleep while you're at it, everyone wins.

Business trips can also be just the break you need to gain perspective on your life at home. When actress Susan Yeagley was hired to do a four-day film shoot in Colorado just months after she had her baby, her doctor advised against it. Susan had been suffering from postpartum depression, and as she describes it, "I was sleep-deprived, shell-shocked, and my lower half looked like I had been in a car accident." But Susan took the job anyway, crediting her return with a mental breakthrough. "It was the single act of going back to work, something I truly loved, that jetted me into being 'unstuck.' Those few days away on set gave me perspective, balance, creativity, and, yes, much-needed rest."

What happens when your worst fears come true and something goes unexpectedly wrong at home while you are away? Morra Aarons-Mele went on a business trip while pregnant with her third child, leaving her two children at home with the nanny because her husband was traveling for work too. While she was away, her nanny called with terrible news; her dog had been run over by a car. Heartbroken, Morra instituted a new nonnegotiable in her life: that would be the last time that she and her husband were both traveling at the same time.

For Tory Johnson, it was a call home to check in that sent her business trip to Dallas into a potential free fall. Her nanny picked up the phone and tearfully explained that the paramedics were there because her 5-year-old son, Jake had cut himself with the kitchen knife. Tory tracked down her husband, Peter, who met their son at the hospital. It was an hour before Tory heard from them. Jake ended up with 12 stitches in his hand. Peter took the next day off from work, and he and Tory together decided that she should stay in Dallas and make it through the event she was running; the work headaches she would create by heading home early were simply not worth it. With one parent home, Jake was more than fine.

Tory finished her event and was home within 24 hours. "I wanted to be home so badly," she explained, "but my presence there would've disappointed too many clients and upset an event that was six months in the making. The only scar that remains is the one on Jake's thumb (and he loves the scar). Nobody remembers that I wasn't there." Tory had the key ingredients she needed to get through this crisis: a dependable partner at home, a guilt-free mentality about her work, and the strength not to let her immediate emotions dictate how she handled the unexpected.

Stop Apologizing to Your Kids

I once had three families over for dinner and was stunned when one of the women, a stay-at-home mom, asked a working mom at the table what she did. Her 10-year-old daughter and I were both listening. I cringed as the working mom said, "Unfortunately, I work." What a missed opportunity for this mom to show her daughter that she was proud of what she does. And it was far from the truth. I know this mom well and I know that she loves her career and would never dream of giving it up. Still, faced with a mom who had made different choices, she felt compelled to apologize and downplay the importance of her job. One of the best pieces of advice I can give you is to *never, ever* apologize for working. I hope you are a mom who enjoys what she does and feels fulfilled by it while contributing financially to the family. To boot, you are a role model to your kids. Why would you ever apologize for that?

Bring Your Kids to Work (Figuratively!)

I will never forget the time that my husband and I were involved in a discussion about my company logo. I had hardly noticed that our then 5-year-old daughter, Ella, was in the room listening. An hour later, she returned to my office and handed me a sheet of paper. It was filled with four designs that she had created, one of which was the inspiration for the final logo. She felt proud, and I felt even prouder.

When an author comes to Ella's school to give a talk, she will often approach him or her and say, "My mom is an author too." She loves my work and feels proud of my success. The ripple effects of this are enormous. When I go on a business trip, my kids do not protest. Instead, they ask where I will be and what I will be doing. I happily share it all with them.

Recently, I had to miss my 7-year-old's dance performance, and she was giving me a very hard time about it. Before I could respond, my 9-year-old chimed in and said, "Ruby, Mommy is at most things." I felt so relieved and grateful.

Far from apologizing, Laura Slabin, Director of Local Content and Community at Google tells her two children that she studied hard in school and worked hard to have her job so she "needs their support." She explains this to mean that they shouldn't cry when she leaves in the morning. Her 3-year-old will often say, "I not cry. I supportive."

When Darian Jennings, a Los Angeles–based mom, went back to work after a few years at home, she experienced the typical concerns and guilt. Would her kids resent her? Would the change impact them negatively? Darian was starting her own company selling her custom-designed cupcakes, cakes, and cookies. Since she was working from home, her kids had a front row seat to watching her business grow, and they often helped out with baking, ribbon cutting for packaging, and many other details involved in getting orders out the door.

Darian's new business was thriving, but she still doubted herself at times, wondering if her kids would be bothered because she wouldn't be available every day after school as she had been before launching the business. Her answer came last summer when she was traveling on vacation with her family.

As they entered a New York bakery, her 8-year-old son, Alex, turned to Darian and exclaimed with pride, "Mommy, this is going to be you some day!" He had been watching his mom baking and delivering orders for months and he was thinking about how she could expand her business. At that moment, Darian dropped the guilt and realized that she was serving as a role model to her kids. She felt a new energy and ambition for her business.

Drawing Lines Around Your Work Life

To manage your life at work, you need to take control of your lifestyle and draw a whole lot of lines. Figure out the nonnegotiables, and start drawing the boundaries at home and at work—whether you are in corporate America or working from home. The more proactive you are about drawing boundaries, the more successful you will be—with your clients, your colleagues, and your loved ones. Boundaries will not only make your life more predictable and less stressful,

---

MANTRAS FROM SUPERWOMEN

"Wake up, kick ass, be nice to people, repeat."

— Gregg Renfrew, founder and CEO, Beauty Counter

"Nobody's coming—it's up to me."

— Tory Johnson, *Good Morning America* contributor

"The patient is waiting." It reminds me to think of those in need and to act with urgency.

— Sally Susman, vice president, Pfizer

"Look out for number one!" If I don't take care of myself and do what makes me happy, I won't be able to make anyone else happy.

— Audrey Puente, meteorologist

"Start your day before the sun does."

— Stacey Bendet, CEO and creative director, Alice and Olivia

"I have to take care of myself so that I can take better care of others."

— Amy Wechsler, dermatologist

"Never give up, never look down, and never look back."

—Samantha Yanks, editor-in-chief

"Leave all the bad stuff in the rear view mirror. Just move on."

—Jane Condon, comedian

"It's chess, not checkers."

—Leslie Hale, chief financial officer, RLJ Lodging Trust

---

they will reduce the number of daily decisions you need to make, allowing you to save your energy for where you need it most.

You now have all the ingredients you need to make work *work*! Whether it is finding a company that you absolutely love or getting the most out of your existing situation, you are the baker and while the recipe won't always be easy, you have all the tools you need to manage a successful work life.

In the next chapter we will talk about another critical ingredient: how to make the most of your time, including tips and tricks that will make you feel like you have an entire extra hour each and every day.

CHAPTER SIX

THE 25TH HOUR

All great achievements require time.

— Maya Angelou

It was 8:34 in the morning, and even though I was sitting in a chilly outdoor theater in Los Angeles, I felt beads of sweat forming in my armpits. I was anxiously waiting to see my seven-year-old daughter, Ruby, perform in her school play, and the stress was killing me. Ruby was to play the lead in *Chrysanthemum*, based on a story by Kevin Henkes. She was supposed to go on first, at 8:10, and I thought I could catch her performance before darting off to do my nine o'clock live radio show. I had arrived at the theater early and positioned myself strategically in the front row off to the side; that way, I thought, Ruby would see me and the memory of my presence would become etched in her mind, and I would still be able to make a quick, unobtrusive escape after she finished her part.

It was now 8:37 and the play still hadn't started. I could make the radio show—the studio was only five minutes from school—but the play needed to start *now*. I found myself wishing that I didn't have to feel so rushed, that I could enjoy my daughter's play and even stay to watch her friends perform. But if I had abruptly canceled that morning's show, I would have risked losing the show altogether. And if I hadn't shown up at my daughter's performance, she and I would have both been devastated. So there I was, trying to fulfill two responsibilities at once, an approach that clearly wasn't working. As I sat there looking for any sign of the kids to emerge, I felt furious with myself for cutting it so close and not anticipating the possibility that her performance could run late. I probably should have just canceled the radio show in advance.

Ruby finally took the stage at 8:41, thirty minutes late. She played her part so beautifully and adorably that for a moment I forgot all about my time crunch. All I wanted to do was grab her and kiss her delicious cheeks, as inviting as the softest pillows—she would always be my baby girl. As soon as she finished, I got up as quietly as I could and raced to my car. As I turned the keys in the ignition, I could barely breathe. All I could think was, "Life shouldn't be lived like this." I sped over to the show, willing myself to stop at every stop sign. With seconds to spare and as the intro music was cueing up, I ran to my chair and put on my headphones. I am shocked that I didn't introduce the show with, "Hello, I am Samantha Ettus and I am about to have a heart attack . . ."

When I ask women across the country to name the one thing they want more of, 90 percent of them say time. The good news is that you can get more time, or at least more useful time. So many minutes slip through our fingers each day, compressing the time we have to devote to people and activities that really matter. I can't magically give you a twenty-fifth hour in your day, but I can share proven strategies for managing your time more effectively so you can win back priceless minutes and hours of your week. If you find a more efficient way to live each day, you will reap the rewards in the form of a much easier life. A key ingredient of any lasting Pie Life makeover is learning how to spend as much time as possible on what matters the most. Adding time to your life will make it easier to have room in your pie for all of the slices. And when we participate in all of the slices, we feel the most fulfilled.

Small Changes Drive Big Results

Did you know that American Airlines once saved $40,000 by removing just *one* olive from each salad tray in first class? It's true. The most minor changes can yield dramatic gains—and not merely in the world of business, but in personal time management as well. To add more time to your life, you don't simply want to look for big, dramatic changes; you also want to pore through your daily schedule to find smaller, seemingly insignificant changes that, over the span of weeks or months, will make a meaningful difference.

Thanks to my work with thousands of women, I've come up with many small tips, techniques, and strategies for managing time better. And in the course of writing this book, I have uncovered still more time-saving secrets that I have adopted in my own life. These tips fall into two categories: general time-savers and more specific tips for streamlining your daily routine. Don't feel the need to instantly incorporate every single one of these strategies into your life—that might be overwhelming. Instead, as you read through the rest of this chapter, circle a few that seem especially accessible and easy. Try them out for a few days or a week, and then come back and pick a few more to work into your life.

Most of us think about budgeting as it pertains to money, but your time can and should be budgeted too. Challenge yourself to constantly up your time management game. Over the course of a month, you'll start to see important changes. And three months in, you'll be marveling at all the newfound time that you have.

The Top Nine Time and Sanity Savers

Strategy #1: Calendar Choreography

I still don't know if "mommy brain" is a myth or a reality, but I do know that if I don't write down an idea or a to-do, it might never return to my mind. After having one too many great gift ideas or scheduling changes or business follow-ups disappear from my memory, I started to write down *everything*. Whether you lean old-school pen and paper or tech-savvy app user, make the calendar your best friend. At the start of the school year, look at your child's school calendar and add every single important item to your own calendar, including holidays, school performances, and parent-teacher conferences. If you have a partner, make sure they add it to theirs too.

Adding the school calendar events to your calendar is important because it affords you the ability to schedule your year *proactively*. You can arrange child care to cover school holidays that you don't have off, you can plan family vacations ahead of time, and most importantly, you can avoid scheduling business trips on days when there are conferences or performances.

So often when we are participating in a conference call, the conversation turns to scheduling and someone asks, "Which two days in October are best for that business trip to Seattle?" If you have the school events already marked on your calendar, you can navigate around those precious days by proactively suggesting alternative dates that work for you.

Strategy #2: Weekly Playdates

One of my favorite tricks as a working parent is to find a family with kids the same age as mine and schedule a weekly playdate, ideally extending through dinner. When my oldest was three years old, I started this kind of arrangement with another family across the street in New York City. I never felt guilty working late on Wednesdays because I knew my kids were having a great time enjoying a playdate and dinner with their friends. Every other Wednesday it was our turn to host, and our sitter supervised the playdate and served dinner while I got a few extra hours to work.

Playdates outside of school are a great boost to your kids' social lives, yet scheduling them can be ridiculously difficult. Working moms don't have time to schedule two new playdates each week per child—coordinating schedules with other parents, making sure our kids are compatible, checking if the other child has food allergies. Reinventing the wheel each week for playdates will send you into an administrative and thankless tailspin. The weekly playdate is the solution: organize it once, and you can rest easy for months without having to reinvent the wheel. A winning byproduct of the consistency is that you have created a more meaningful friendship at the same time.

Strategy #3: The Golden Triangle

Here's a great shortcut that seems so obvious you'll wonder why you didn't think of it. To get back some of your lost time each week, commit to doing all of your errands—from hair to groceries to doctors' appointments—within what I call "the Golden Triangle." This is a triangle defined by three points: your workplace, your home, and your child's school. You have to drive or walk between these points anyway throughout your week or even every day, so you might as well take the opportunity to perform errands along the way. If you commit to trading your out-of-the-way hair stylist, markets, and dentist for those within the triangle, you will save hours each month.

I know you might be wed to your favorite hairstylist or dermatologist whose office is 20 miles away, but I assure you that talented people exist within your triangle. You can (and must!) find them.

When I first relocated my family to Los Angeles, one of my greatest challenges was finding the right people, from the pediatrician to the plumber, who could be part of our team. After a mishap that nearly resulted in my daughter undergoing an unnecessary dental procedure, a friend sent me for a second opinion to her relative, a pediatric dentist one hour from my home. My need for an honest dentist had me doing this one-hour drive for two years. I would schedule all three kids' appointments at once and we would make a Saturday road trip out of it.

All went well until my son got sick on the day of the kids' teeth cleaning. I brought the girls and then had to return separately with my son. Six months later, it was my daughter who came down with a stomach bug on the day of the dental visit. Again, I had to make two trips. I realized that there had to be a

TIME-SAVERS FROM WOMEN WHO KNOW

"Take-out meals are made by people too and you heat them up at home, so technically they are homemade meals!"

—Kathleen Schmidt, associate publisher

"Don't straighten your hair—it takes too much time, and curly is more fun anyway!"

—Mandee Heller Adler, founder and president, International College Counselors

"Hire a personal assistant. I put an ad at my local college advertising the need for someone to run errands and organize my house. She picks up my dry cleaning, changes batteries in the fire alarms, registers kids for activities, purchases and wraps gifts, and hundreds of other mundane tasks."

—Jessica Stokes, Innovation Operations Leader, Ernst & Young

"Set up a monthly shipment for your regular household products like paper goods, cleaning supplies, toiletries, etc. Programs like Amazon Prime offer free shipping."

—Nadine Zysman, elementary school vice principal

"When going away for the weekend, keep a tote in your home at the ready so that during the week you can add at your leisure what you want to bring away. Then there isn't the last minute racing to pack and dash. You leave for the weekend feeling relaxed."

—Samantha Yanks, editor-in-chief, *Hamptons* magazine

more local solution. And there was: our new dentist is five minutes from home and sits all three kids in chairs right next to one another. They are even worked on all at once by her and her hygienists—an efficiency fantasy!

Julia, a photographer and mother of two, swore she would never leave her hair colorist even though her salon was an hour's drive from her home. Julia went there every four weeks—that is, until she did the math. She lived in a big city with a salon on every block and realized that if she could find a good hair colorist within 10 minutes of her home, she would save more than 90 minutes a month. That would add up to an entire *day* per year. She switched and hasn't looked back. (And don't tell her old stylist, but her hair looks better than ever!)

Strategy #4: Craft the Commutes

In an ideal world, you would stumble out of bed, head into your office across the street, and send your children to school around the corner. For most of America, this isn't realistic. Many of us commute to our jobs—30 minutes, an hour, even longer. The average commute in America is 26 minutes each way, or almost an hour a day. More than 10 million Americans commute over two hours a day.[17]

It's easy to write off the time we spend commuting as wasted or "down" time. Try instead viewing that time as "usable hours." If you are commuting via bus or train, use the time to return e-mails or work on a presentation. If you are in a car, use the time to return (hands-free) phone calls, catch up on news, or listen to audiobooks. You might also try using the time to stay connected with friends and former colleagues.

As for the kids' school commutes, you want to minimize those. When it came time to choose a Manhattan preschool for our daughter Ella, we chose one across the street. Were there better schools in New York? Perhaps. We chose the school largely based on geography. We ended up super happy there—it was a lovely, warm start to her education, and a big part of what made it so wonderful was the one-block commute. Ella turned it into a daily 20-minute excursion, taking time to notice the snow on awnings and new birds and a crowded bus stop. I tried to make sure we had time for this each day but even when we didn't, the one block made it so that we didn't have to rush.

The early years are physically demanding for parents, and the more you can do to make them easier, the more you'll enjoy them. I always think geography should be the number one factor in identifying a preschool or day care. There is likely at least a "good enough" school—and probably an excellent one—that doesn't require 40 minutes of travel time. Find it.

Strategy #5: Decide Fast and Don't Look Back

Every day we make numerous decisions, both big and small. Here are some of the issues I needed to resolve on a single Tuesday recently: Do I book the flight that arrives the night before or the morning of my next speaking gig? Do I cook dinner that night or order in? Does my daughter need a new tennis racket? Do I stay up another hour to respond to e-mails or get the extra hour of sleep? Do I let my son stay at his friend's house for dinner or pick him up so we can eat as a family?

These constant decisions can consume us if we let them. We think that the more time we spend muddling over the pros and cons, the better our decisions will be. Nonsense. Thinking through a decision is important up to a point, but after that, the returns diminish. Be bold. Decide quickly and move forward! Here is how I handled my decisions that day: Do I book the flight that arrives the night before or the morning of my next speaking gig? The night before! Do I cook dinner that night or order in? Order in! Does my daughter need a new tennis racket? Delay buying until next year! Do I stay up another hour to respond to e-mails or get the extra hour of sleep? Sleep! Do I let my son stay at his friend's house for dinner or pick him up so we can eat as a family? Let him stay!

Don't look back, and never beat yourself up for choosing an option that didn't work so well. Simply incorporate what you've learned into your future decision making.

Strategy #6: The Gift Stash

After receiving one too many last-minute invitations to birthday parties, I began keeping a gift stash for grown-ups *and* kids, things like my favorite books or children's games all wrapped and ready to go. That way, my family and I would never again have to show up at a friend's house empty-handed and we avoid the extra errand of buying a gift. At the beginning of the year, when the stores are running their big sales, buy a bunch of age-appropriate birthday presents— about 10 of each so that a kid's birthday party doesn't become a giant, looming errand. Sue, an attorney from Atlanta does this with cards too. "Once a year I buy a big box of variety cards so that every time I need a birthday or wedding card, I already have it." Sure it would be nice to buy cards and gifts as needed so that we could make them super personal. But when it comes down to it, avoiding the last-minute gift scramble is well worth it.

Strategy #7: Outsource to Your Kids

When we feel rushed, we tend to do things for our kids in the interests of speed (e.g., packing her backpack, tying his shoelaces), telling ourselves that we'll let our kids do it on their own next time. But when we helicopter like that, we stifle independence. And guess what? The short-term pain of waiting the extra minute for your daughter to pack her own backpack or your son to tie his shoelace is time well spent so that you can reap the future gains. Actress Autumn Reeser explains, "As a single mom, the more I can delegate to my little ones, the less hectic mornings are." Figure out age-appropriate activities your kids can do on their own. Get dressed? Pour cereal? Once the skills are learned you will save time, and in the meantime, you'll also help your kids gain confidence, and move toward independence.

Many parents not only helicopter their kids; they also burden themselves with the myth of "quality time." We define quality time narrowly as "doing something fun together," and we forget that when we simply pay attention to our kids, we become their favorite toys. A trip to the supermarket always delighted my then 4-year-old son. He would sit in the cart, and we talked about the list and what we would cook together. He especially loved that he got to pick a "cookie of the week." In the meantime, I had checked a big item off my to-do list and had a great time with my child. Kids love your phone-free attention, and it doesn't require having an endless tea party on the rug. A trip to the drug store or the bank can be quality time. Never fill your gas tank without your kids, and the same goes for the car wash. Like many things in life, errands are all about how you present them. If you say, "Let's go to the supermarket and you will be in charge of the list," or "Let's go get the ingredients for your favorite lasagna," the activity suddenly sounds a lot less like a chore and a lot more like fun.

Strategy #8: Use the Rules

Schools, day-care facilities, gyms—they all have rules. Make sure you're using them to your advantage. Your preschool has a 15-minute drop-off window? Drop your kids off at the beginning of the window and win an extra 15 minutes each day. You will feel less rushed and your child will benefit from the more comfortable transition of seeing the room fill up rather than entering an already full classroom.

Strategy #9: Recurring Events

For me, there is nothing worse than losing two hours scrambling at the last minute for a babysitter, or calling the salon just before a TV appearance and hearing that they can't fit me in. Booking last minute for recurring events is a reliable way to waste untold amounts of time. So stop and think ahead about what events in your life might be recurring. Since I was 19 years old, I have had gray hairs. Only a few strands then, many more now. Since my work requires TV and in-person appearances, I cannot afford to go more than three weeks without getting my hair colored. Yet for years, I behaved as though my hair coloring was an unpredictable item that came up when I looked in the mirror and noticed the grays. Today I don't leave the salon without booking for next time. The same thing goes for our weekly Saturday night sitter. Instead of calling around at the last minute each week, we have her booked.

Streamlining Your Daily Routine

Now that you have my general time-saving techniques, let's win back more time by looking more closely at your daily routines. You will soon realize that even the smallest of changes will shave minutes off your day and add energy to your tank.

Daily Strategy #1: Be a Triathlete

How many mornings do you leave the house to take your kids to school and then need to go back for things you left behind? Amid all the stress, what happens? Do you raise your voice or get impatient with your kids? What you're struggling with here is the *transition* between home and school. It's critically important to get these transitions right. As triathletes will tell you, races are won and lost in the transition between the running, the swimming, and the biking. Your day will be "won" or "lost" in the transitions as well. So how do you make transitions successful? Most of it comes down to preparation:

The Night Before

Every night, set aside 10 minutes to pick out your clothes for the next day and clothes for your small children (if your kids are ages 5 or older, they can pick out their own). Also use this time to set the table for the next morning's breakfast. Nonprofit CEO Sheila Michail Morovati likes to pack dinner leftovers in a thermos the night before and then warm them up in the morning to have for lunch. Michele Costa, full-time working mom of three kids, has to drop her kids at the sitter in time to make her 7:11 commuter train. She does it by putting her kids to sleep in their clothes for the next day. "It's a real lifesaver for me," she says, and I agree. My third-grade daughter was having trouble waking up in the mornings, so she started going to sleep in her school uniform—luckily it is a comfortable and wrinkle-free one! This made the morning routine much faster and less stressful for her. Since then she has dropped this unusual habit (Mom is grateful) but that year, it served her needs.

The Mornings

If you're like me, you find that unexpected developments can eat up your mornings. Your son has a headache or needs some extra TLC. Your daughter forgets to do the last part of her Spanish homework. The babysitter calls in sick. You need to get to the office to handle a crisis. Many aspects of daily life are out of our control, but we can handle them much more effectively if we organize the areas of our lives that we *can* control.

Take advantage of what I call the "Magic Hour." This is the blissful hour in the morning before your kids' alarms go off—when you can get yourself showered, dressed, and ready for the day at a pace that is human! When I counseled Dina, an overwhelmed mother of three, she couldn't find a way to take control of her mornings. No matter what she promised herself, by 7:00 a.m. she felt like a dog chasing her own tail and found herself taking it out on her kids. Once she committed to going to bed an hour earlier and waking before her kids to shower, get dressed, and make the family breakfast, she felt like a champion. In short order, she found herself becoming far more patient with her children and yelling far less.

Another important tactic to keep in mind is to make sure your "supplies" are all in the right places. Every member of your family needs his or her own equivalent of a cubby, and their backpack, lunchbox, homework, sports equipment, musical instrument, and shoes all need to live there. This means you won't lose time looking for lost items, and your kids will know exactly where to put stuff when they get home for school. When everything has its place, life becomes easier for everyone.

Daily Strategy #2: Deal with Meals

I once spoke to a room full of executives who were brought to tears talking about the challenges of coming up with family dinners five nights a week. For many women, myself included, menu planning is one of the hardest parts of being a working mom. But it gets way worse when you don't plan in advance. I recommend that you sit down and regularly plan meals for the entire week. Every Sunday, enlist your kids' help, make at least three dishes for the week, and freeze them. I'm not talking about hours of drudgery—I'm talking about "Sunday afternoon cooking parties!"

Whether or not you do cooking parties, cookbook author Katie Workman recommends setting your sights on two to four home-cooked meals for your kids each week. It's kind of like exercising: when we aim for all seven days, we can find ourselves not doing it at all, but when we have a manageable goal like two to four times a week, we can make it happen. Workman recommends doing pasta on one night, stir-fry on another, and a simple chicken dish on the third. All of this becomes easier if you do your prep on the weekends. Mince garlic and chop onions, for instance, and store them in your fridge. That way when you need them during the week, they'll be ready to use.

Laurie David, author of *The Family Cooks,* recommends that you turn over the making of salad dressing to one of your children. "It takes only three or four ingredients to make a healthy and delicious dressing, yet the store-bought kinds have dozens of ingredients. For a healthier and inexpensive alternative, make your own and assign this fun task to one of your kids! They will love taking ownership of this important family job and will grow up always preferring homemade to store-bought. You can make enough on Sunday to last your whole week long."

You can also ease the burden on yourself by doing "brinner" (breakfast for dinner) one night a week. Kids think it's fun, and whipping up eggs only takes five minutes.

And then there are lunchboxes. I vividly remember the feeling I had when I put together my first lunchbox: I was so excited to have a child who was old enough to eat lunch in school. It seemed as big a milestone as losing a first tooth. That beautiful first lunchbox had hummus, carrots, a tuna sandwich, a hard-boiled egg, and some sliced strawberries. I was beaming with pride so I did what any social media lover would do—I posted it on Facebook.

I will never forget what my friend Suzy said: "You will be dreading those lunchboxes before you know it." Sadly, that day came quicker than I expected. I had three lunchboxes to make every day and each child demanded different items. One liked sunflower butter and jelly, another wouldn't touch it. One couldn't stand hummus and one had to have it. Keeping track of my kids' varied tastes and preferences and then delivering them was endlessly stressful and time consuming.

When my husband took over morning kitchen duty recently, he also took over lunchboxes. I felt a huge wave of relief. There are some things we now do to make lunchboxes easier. First, we keep freshly sliced fruit in glass containers in the fridge at all times. They are easy lunchbox fillers and double as perfect snacks when the kids get home from school or practice. I also learned a great trick from Tanya Yarbrough, a Tennessee-based mom of two and professional homebuilder: "My kids each had two lunch boxes. We packed lunch Sunday night for Monday and Tuesday and Tuesday night for Wednesday and Thursday. On Friday they had school lunch. This cut lunch prep from four times a week to two."

Daily Strategy #3: Dress for Success

Sitting and staring at your closet each morning is a colossal waste of time and energy. Fashion designer Liz Lange recommends using Sunday nights to look over your schedule for the week and decide what you'll wear each day. She explains, "If I feel that I need to try on anything, I do it Sunday evening so as not to have that morning time suck and panic of nothing to wear. If planning an entire week's worth of outfits on a Sunday night sounds daunting, do it each night for the next day before you go to sleep at night."

Lange also recommends having a go-to look—a style that you know looks good on you—and buying a variety of that dress or pants-and-top combo in different colors. To find your uniform, look at the outfit you instinctively turn to when you have a big meeting or presentation, the one that makes you feel best. "I love dresses," Lange says, "so I have several that I rotate for different occasions. For business, it's usually black, navy, or gray but for personal appearances or TV it's usually a color. I keep my closet grouped by color so it's easy for me to find a blue dress when I'm looking for one. Once you've discovered your uniform, you'll find that you shop more efficiently and have much more time and less stress in the mornings."

Many women make their lives more stressful by getting ready twice. They throw on sweats and a T-shirt, tie their hair in a bun, and dab on some lip gloss before bringing their child to the bus. Then they run home and get ready for their workday. This is a giant waste of time. Unless you are working out, skip the initial outfit and shower before you leave the house the first time. Get ready once and hit the day running.

Daily Strategy #4: Be a Superhero

Mornings are messy—literally! Not long ago I ran upstairs to put on some last-minute makeup before taking the kids to school and, as I hear my kids calling my name to tell me they are ready to go, I dripped foundation on my favorite top. Ouch! That incident brought back memories of when my oldest was a baby: I don't think there was a morning that I left the house without a spit stain on my left shoulder. New York–based editor Gabrielle Birkner shares this genius tip: "Buy one of those capes that salons use when they cut your hair and cover your clothes with it until you are ready to walk out the door." Wearing a cape ensures that lunchbox and breakfast prep are no longer outfit-threatening endeavors.

MORE TIME-SAVERS FROM WOMEN WHO KNOW

"Have a bunch of recipes that can each be pulled together in 30 minutes or less."

— Debora Spar, president of Barnard College

"Use your commute time as 'me' time to let your mind grapple with a work problem so you can put it away later, talk on the phone, listen to music, or listen to an audiobook. It's important to position the time that it takes to get between work and home as a positive bridge versus a chore."

—Marisa Thalberg, chief marketing officer,
Taco Bell

"When I go to the gym in the morning, I bring my clothes there so I can shower and go straight to work. I save almost an hour that way.

—Ramy Sharp, CEO and creative director,
Ramy Brook

"No one looks in the trunk of your car. Throw the mess back there and get on with your life."

—Susan Yeagley, actress

"Choose things that make life more convenient . . . classes and schools close by, and work that is ideally close to home."

—Laura Slabin, director of local content
and community, Google

Time Changes

Good time management comes down to preparation and being a step ahead of the game rather than a step behind. If you go to sleep with the outfits picked out, the backpacks packed, the table set, and your to-do list written out, you are practically guaranteed to hit the ground running. Add in meal planning, weekly playdates, and regular appointments with sitters and you are cruising. If you can top it off with some big-picture adjustments like doing your errands within the Golden Triangle, using the Magic Hour, making faster decisions, relying on your gift stash, and fostering your kids' independence so they can contribute, you can feel great about having made the absolute most of your time.

So much of our ability to handle the unexpected depends on our ability to manage the things that are under our control. Since that frenzied morning when my daughter's play nearly conflicted with my radio show, I've realized that I need to plan for the unexpected. Running a repeat show would have been fine if I had let my producers know about it in advance. When we run our lives more efficiently, we are happier and more relaxed—we just *feel* better.

Remember that scene in *I Love Lucy* where Ethel and Lucy are working in the candy factory and they can't keep up with the assembly line that's producing all the chocolates? The scene was all about operations failure. Lucy tries to fix the assembly line—unsuccessfully—by shoving chocolates in her mouth as they come off the line. The scene is funny, but it also suggests a serious point: when we feel spread in many directions, we fail at even the basics. It pays to have our operations down pat.

That said, hiccups will arise. You won't ever be free from mistakes and when they occur, the best thing you can do is laugh and learn. These things happen to everyone and I have proof. In the fall of 2014 I was speaking at a Club MomMe event on a work/life balance panel moderated by journalist Lisa Ling, who I have always admired for her confidence and poise but most of all for her ability to get to the bottom of a story. If the term "bad ass" needed a poster girl, I would nominate Lisa.

The panel was on a Sunday afternoon and when I chatted with the other panelists before it began, we all seemed to have partners or parents at home who were spending the day with the kids so we could be there. As Lisa was asking one of the questions, she shared her own work/life mishap. She had shown up for this event the previous day because she had added it to her calendar incorrectly. So she left her daughter on a Saturday, got all dressed up, drove the hour to get to the conference, and upon arrival, discovered nobody was there. She had lost not one of her weekend days with her child but both, and when she shared this story, you could see that she was still beating herself up over it. The audience and the panelists lapped it up because we could all relate. Lisa Ling—she is just like us. We all have these experiences, but our ability to bounce back from them fast is based on the value we apply to them. They are mere moments, and if they are symbolic of anything it is that we are human and prone to make errors—even at our best.

By making your daily life more efficient, you will have a bit more time to dig into all of your slices. In the next chapter, we will learn how to create and maintain a village. If you already have one, let's make it even stronger. If you don't yet have yours, let's go find it.

CHAPTER SEVEN

THE VILLAGE

Alone we can do so little; together we can do so much.

— Helen Keller

Any parent who relocates to a new city or town without extended family nearby will confirm the panic that sets in when you are asked to list two emergency contacts who are not your spouse. Looking down at that form and having no names to write down in those boxes is one of the loneliest feelings. Our first year in Los Angeles, I had to provide contact information at two schools. Wracking my brain and going back and forth on the topic with Mitch, we finally settled on two old friends who had met our kids only once or twice and lived more than an hour away. It wasn't much, but it was the best we could do. After that, I set a goal for myself: I would build a network and make local friends so that, within a year, we would have no trouble filling out the emergency contact list (and I would have some great women to enjoy!).

You can't work, enjoy date nights, run a home, and raise well-adjusted kids without a village. It used to be that we all lived within yards of extended family to help us out. Now that this is no longer the norm, you need to put in hard work to create a support network. Chances are you have already started to build one. Perhaps you have a sibling nearby, a couple of close friends, a great sitter, and a good work friend that you can count on out of the office. But let's say you are like I was a few years ago—in an unfamiliar city, lacking even a single nearby friend or acquaintance.

While I was working hard to get us settled at school and in our new home, I knew that my feeling of security and comfort in my new city would not arrive until I again felt the safety net of a village surrounding me. I went about this the same way I had gone about finding a life partner—proactively. And it wouldn't be long before I had to tap into it.

Mitch started his last company, a small business lender, at our kitchen table. We had no savings at the time, and we needed this to be a winner, so I pitched in to help. I named the company (On Deck Capital), made its first cold calls, and hired the initial sales team. It was never easy—the life of an entrepreneur is a roller coaster, and the days of company building can feel like the slow, creaky cars struggling to get to the top of that first big hill. Investors came and went, product hiccups came to light, a sales manager left one night and never returned—you get the picture. But Mitch persevered and the company took root. For the first year or two, it was our baby, but after that, I stepped back and Mitch grew and ran the company himself. Years later, eager to start his next venture, he sold most of his stake and shifted the CEO title to his number two.

In 2014, the company Mitch had founded was expected to go public. After months of anticipation, we finally received the date for this momentous occasion: "Join us in New York to ring the starting bell," the invitation read, to signify the opening of the stock market at the New York Stock Exchange on December 17. He was delighted; it was the stuff of entrepreneurial dreams and as the visionary behind the company, he was thrilled at its ongoing success.

We both assumed I would join him on the trip to mark this moment. With Mitch looking over my shoulder, I opened up the calendar. "Bowen's holiday party" was on the very same day. No! This annual party was a three-hour celebration in my son's classroom that required one parent or family member to attend. I had joined Bowen at the party for the previous two years, and I knew how important it was for each child to have a parent there. Tears came to my eyes. "Well," I said to Mitch, "looks like you'll be going alone."

Mitch suggested we take a few days to think it over. That Friday night, we went to a regular monthly dinner we hold with four families. The kids were off playing and the parents were chatting. I mentioned to my four mom friends how disappointed I was at having to miss such an important milestone in Mitch's life and in *our* life. "This is crazy!" my friend Nadine said. "You are not missing it just so you can go to a three-hour preschool holiday party. Bowen knows me very well. I am going in your place and we will have a ball."

Tears came to my eyes. "That's so kind of you, but no, I can't let you do that."

"Of course you can," she said. "I absolutely insist."

I was touched by my friend's concern, and I appreciated her pointing out how insane I was to even contemplate missing this huge event. I also felt a sense of pride at having a friend like Nadine in my life. Just like Mitch hadn't fallen into my lap on the dating scene, neither had she. We had worked hard to build up a social network for ourselves, good friends we could count on—a village. I thought we had been making headway, but I had yet to rely on our network for anything significant. And here was Nadine offering to fill in as a family member so I could be at Mitch's side for a once-in-a-lifetime milestone. I took her up on it. This was further evidence that even though friends are only one slice of your pie, they have the ability to impact all the other slices.

My story pales in comparison to that of Emme Kozloff, finance executive and mom of two, who was diagnosed with breast cancer in 2014. She describes friends who would bring food on days when she had chemo and it was too much for her husband to take care of her and the kids at the same time. Explains Emme, "I am more of a private person so it was a small, tight village." She describes these people as the ones she could call in the middle of the night to show up if she needed them.

Date Smart

How do you create social networks like these? First, start meeting other moms, and not just any moms—the *right* ones. During my first year in Los Angeles, I went on about 100 "first dates" with other moms who I thought could be part of my support network. I said yes to every invitation I received, whether it was from a friend of a friend, a woman in line at Starbucks who liked my scarf—anyone. I was driven in large part by desperation.

The energy and openness I was putting into creating a village was great, but after six to nine months, I was making only limited headway. I had met a few friends, but nobody I felt strongly about, and nobody I thought I could really count on if push came to shove. I soon realized my mistake: I was trying to form new relationships without applying any kind of filter.

Most people know that when you date romantically, you need a filter. When you were single, would you have accepted a date with someone who lived 100 miles from you, was allergic to your pet, and liked to spend late nights seeing live music while you preferred reading at home? No! That first year, I wasted so much time having coffee, drinks, or lunches with women who shared little in common with me. Their kids weren't close to my children's ages, they lived more than 30 minutes away, and they didn't work. Given my commitments to my young kids, my marriage, and my career, it was unlikely that I would be traveling a half hour without my family to see these women for a second date.

If I was going to build a village, I had to work smarter and more efficiently. So during my second year in Los Angeles, I began investing in potential friendships with women who were either local, had kids the same age, or had similar business interests. If a woman didn't have any of these three criteria, I wouldn't make a date with her, since I felt pretty confident that given the logistical constraints, she would never be part of my village. By pursuing potential friendships more selectively, I had a much higher rate of success. In no time, I was meeting women whom I really liked. The next big challenge was finding time to see them again and turning the acquaintance into friendship.

The Home Team

Good friends on whom you can rely may comprise the core of your village, but other people must be part of it too. When you first move to a new city, start building what I call a "home team" consisting of a plumber, electrician, handyman, and so on—all of the people you would need in case of a home emergency. Trust me; you'll be glad you did.

During our first date night after moving into our house, we were out to dinner when my phone rang with a hysterical call from our new babysitter, Noelle: a pipe had burst under the kitchen sink and our night out along with it. Noelle's desperate efforts to clog up the hole with towels was no match for the geyser that was remodeling our new kitchen. Check please! Fortunately, I had already assembled an initial roster for my home team. I called the plumber from the restaurant, whose number was already in my phone, and even though it was a Saturday night, he made it to our house before we did. Despite our panic as we raced down the Pacific Coast Highway, a small part of me felt like a cocky superhero knowing that I was prepared for this moment. Instead of being greeted by thousands of dollars of water damage, we were greeted by our plumber's rear end. Not the romantic evening I had envisioned, but it could have been a lot worse.

Between our careers and our roles as parents, our lives are too busy for a house calamity like this to turn into a two-week project; we simply don't have the time and neither do you. The home team prevents your time from disappearing reactively whenever something unexpected happens. It requires so little time to assemble and saves you so much time later on.

WHO'S IN *YOUR* VILLAGE?

Two or more mom friends you can count on:

_____

_____

_____

A primary child-care provider (nanny, babysitter, family member) plus two backups:

_____

_____

_____

_____

Two reliable neighbors:

_____

_____

The home team:

Electrician _____

Carpenter _____

Plumber _____

Handyman _____

Exterminator_____

Other _____

Other _____

The medical team:

Preferred emergency room _____

Primary Care _____

Pediatrician _____

Dentist _____

Specialist _____

Dermatologist _____

Other _____

Your home team will likely be a work in progress. To compile an initial roster, ask new coworkers, friends, and neighbors to recommend anyone you might need—an exterminator, an electrician, someone reliable to shovel your driveway in the winter. As you meet more people and hear about their favorite tradespeople and other vendors, add them to the list.

Besides a home team, you should also start assembling two other critically important teams. First, there's the child-care team: babysitters, au pairs, or nannies. It doesn't matter what you call them, it only matters that you trust them with your precious children. If you think home child care is elitist, think again! There are a range of options, and people all around the world make use of caregivers. In households with two big careers, day care often won't cut it because workday schedules do not typically conform to a child-care facility's schedule. Even if they do, a nanny or au pair (typically a young woman from another country who exchanges child care for room and board as well as a small stipend) allows for more career flexibility because parents have less to worry about at home.

For years, sales executive Felicia Alexander counted two nannies as an integral part of her village. She and her husband both worked, and there was no other way to get everything done while assuring the best care for the couple's son. As time passed and their son got older, the couple largely phased out the nannies, rotating in some "energetic college students" to provide babysitting help. Yet the nannies have remained members of the family's village.

A second team that should form part of your family's village is the "doctor team." When a member of your family experiences a medical emergency, there's nothing better than having a trusted doctor on speed dial. Anyone who cares for your child, whether it's you, your partner, your sitter, your assistant, or your mother-in-law, should all have your doctors' numbers in their phones. They should also know which emergency room you would want them to choose, if it comes to that. These are not pleasant things to think about, but when you are prepared to handle natural disasters—whether home calamities or medical problems—you end up avoiding a bigger issue that can take all of your slices down with it.

Five years ago, Allison, a San Francisco mom of three, collapsed and couldn't pick herself off the floor. She was crippled by severe anxiety, all the more puzzling since she had no family history of it. Over the next two years, Allison got back on her feet with the help of a team of doctors assembled by her mother.

Only two years later, Allison found herself calling upon this team again, this time to help her son with a similar anxiety attack. Allison related to me how heartbreaking her son's anxiety was, but also how fortunate she felt to already have a team waiting to help. "The only silver lining I can see to the struggle I went through for two years is that I could empathize completely with my child. I am so proud of him and happy to say that with the right team, we had him back on track within a couple of weeks." Having her mental health team on speed dial meant the difference between years of suffering for Allison's son, or an isolated episode of anxiety that was contained within just a few weeks.

You might have an eye issue come up and not have an ophthalmologist at your fingertips, but as long as you have a primary care physician you trust, she or he can recommend the right specialists immediately. Choose your medical team carefully and wisely, not just for talent and experience, but also for proximity and responsiveness. Your insurance plan might not always give you as many options as you would like, but it is worthwhile to research the choices you do have. If your doctor takes three days to return your call, it might be time to search for a new one.

Two-Mom Insurance

To build the best possible village for yourself, you must take your efforts to the next level and go hunting. Not deer hunting. Not rabbit hunting. *Mom* hunting.

You know those "two or more mom friends" on the list on page 109? You can find them by going on many first "dates" (filter on!) with other moms. But a powerful shortcut is to identify two moms in each of your kids' grades that you think might make good friends and set up coffee with them. By "friends," I don't mean you need to tell one another your deepest secrets or go on regular "girls weekends" together. That might eventually happen, but for now, let's just find some moms whom you can feel comfortable calling for a ride to a soccer game or advice on what your child should wear to the school dance. Even if you have family nearby, you'll have days when your child is sick and you need to call another parent for the homework assignment, or days when a work crisis has come up and you need to arrange a ride for your child to a birthday party. These are the friends that can step up on those occasions, and of course you would reciprocate when they need you.

You could wait for friends like this to strike up relationships with you. Or . . . you could actively recruit them. The strategy:

Target Them

The mistake we tend to make is to look around the school at drop-off and say, "I am not like these parents." Maybe you don't dress alike or have the same accent or share a history. No matter; you need to change your lens. These moms do not need to look like your best friends from college; it's practically a guarantee that they won't. You are looking for parents you can count on and who share your general parenting philosophy. Looking back on it now, I realize that my own radar was often way off the mark initially. I once saw a journalist mom from a distance and assumed she would be my new mom BFF. When we were introduced, we had zero chemistry—like the plus sides of two batteries. Then there were the women I would never have guessed would turn into my trusted friends.

My husband likes to say that you can grow to love anyone if you spend enough time with them, and it turns out, there is science behind this theory: proximity and the frequency of interactions are critical to forming friendships. Along these lines, no matter how busy you are, you will need to devote some time to making and maintaining your friendships.

Interview Them

Take time out of your busy schedule in the beginning of the school year to ask a few potential candidate parents for coffee. Get to know them. Even if they don't wind up among your final two picks, you will have only gained by getting to know more of your child's classmates' parents.

If you get a good feeling from your coffee dates, invite these moms and their families for Sunday night dinner so your kids can meet them too. Finding some chemistry between your families is an important development in the friendship.

Court Them

Once you have selected your "finalists," offer to help *them*. Ask if they might like you to give their kids a ride to practice, or to have their kids over for dinner on a night they're working. You want to be the one who makes the overture first; you never want to have to ask for help before you have helped them. And don't make your offer of help a one-time thing. I have a motto: anytime you can help someone without hurting yourself or your family, do it! So if I'm going to a kid's birthday party or practice, I try to offer a ride to another local family.

I like to help someone at least twice before I need to ask for a favor. That way, if I later find myself in a bind because of a last-minute business trip or a sitter cancellation, I have people to call on who are generally happy to reciprocate. The more you help, the more you can draw upon your own favor bank when you need to—and you never know when you might need to. I don't mean to suggest that a favor back is the only thing you get from this. Helping makes us feel good—it is incredibly gratifying to know that you have assisted another person, which is another reason it is important not to view this as a straight quid pro quo.

When I offered some business advice to Lena, another parent in Bowen's class, over coffee one day, I did so because I like Lena and wanted to help her. I couldn't have imagined that it would make it easier for me to ask her for last-minute child-care help just a few weeks later. It was the day before a business trip (on these days, I try to make a point of picking up my kids from school), and when I went to school to get Bowen, I was startled to learn that there was a day off the next day that had not made it on to my calendar. We had no one to watch him. My husband would be in meetings, I would be on a plane, and our sitter couldn't come until three in the afternoon. I called Lena and she happily agreed to have Bowen over. When you help people, they remember.

Attorney Sahara Pynes has her three kids in after-school activities spread out across Los Angeles. On any given day, she finds it essential to have not only two moms in each of her kids' grades to count on, but also two moms in each after-school activity. That way, she says, "I have a responsible adult to call if I'm running late or stuck in a meeting." Another tactic Sahara uses is to arrange carpools so she can schedule driving days that fit her needs; if she has a trip or a meeting, she can schedule her days around that. This kind of advanced planning is what enables Sahara to work, be an involved parent, and have time for her husband and friends. Several slices of her pie benefit, and the arrangement is practically on autopilot!

Leaning On the Village

Over years of talking and working with women, I've heard so many stories of women whose villages came through for them in the toughest of times. When Tracy relocated with her husband and three children from Mendham,

New Jersey, to Augusta, Georgia, to open a tennis club, she could hardly have anticipated the troubles that would confront her.

Within a year of their arrival, the tennis club business collapsed and her family faced financial ruin. Their home in New Jersey went into foreclosure proceedings, two of their three cars broke down, and their three children were dismissed midyear from the private elementary school they adored for financial reasons. The bills kept piling up as Tracy and her family went further and further into debt. Although Tracy had not yet created her new local village, one new friendship she had formed made an enormous difference. She recalls, "There was one certain dear friend and lady, Jeannie. The emotional and financial support she has so freely given will stay with me forever, and it reminds me that there is good in this world, right along with the bad times. You just have to find it."

In 2013, Kelly Flynn, her husband, and two sons relocated from Boston to Minneapolis, leaving behind their support system, including Kelly's parents and sister. Kelly tried to make new friends but could not have imagined how much she would need them and how soon.

Two years after moving, Kelly suffered a second trimester miscarriage and was devastated. She was already visibly showing, so all of her friends knew that she was pregnant. In the days following the miscarriage, Kelly was so upset that she couldn't help but share her grief with everyone she encountered. If there was a bright spot for Kelly, it was the love her new mom friends and their families showed her. "They made it clear that they cared about me and my family and would help us in any way possible; this was helpful mostly because it was heartwarming and made us feel so loved." Kelly, who didn't usually ask others for help, found herself asking one of her closer friends, "Please check in on me in the coming days." The friend not only came through but exceeded Kelly's expectations by texting her every day to see how she was doing.

Villages aren't just for when the going gets tough. They make life better at *all* times. Finance executive Alexandra Lebenthal counts her sister as a critical part of her children's lives: "We call her the "Par-Aunt" because she has truly been such a part of raising all three of our kids. She never married or had kids of her own, so she was always ready to help with ours. She jumped in at times when we needed her, took them on great trips, and introduced them to so many things."

When we first moved to Los Angeles, I began inviting a new family over every Sunday at three o'clock for a playdate followed by an early dinner. The kids had fun and the grown-ups got to know one another in a low-key environment. Four years after we moved there, we still do these Sunday dinners, sometimes with our "old friends" and sometimes with new families we are just getting to know. These evenings make our village stronger because the parents we invite get to know our children and our family culture well. Our kids gain confidence because they form new friendships outside of school; they also feel proud of our Sunday dinners and look forward to them so much that they often ask early in the week who is coming to dinner the following Sunday.

When Mitch and I went away for a three-night trip last fall, we didn't just rely on our usual sitter to care for our kids. We made plans for the kids to go to various playdates and have dinner at a family friend's home one night so they would feel surrounded by love and activities—and miss us a bit less. We had put our village to great use.

Forming a village requires an ongoing commitment, and it might be some time before you realize the full payback. When we first relocated to the West Coast, Mitch overheard some moms chatting at school about a group they were forming to meet monthly with a local parent educator. Knowing what it would mean for me to be part of a group of women that met regularly, he very pushily suggested they invite me. At the first meeting, I discovered that these women were all close friends already—they had known one another since their kids were infants in a "mommy and me" class. Although I felt like an outsider and was tempted not to return, I stuck with it; after several months, I finally felt like I belonged enough to share my own stories and issues. Years later, I can now say I love these women. So what if they didn't know my kids before they could walk; we've got each other's backs now and I feel so grateful to have them in my life.

The village you create is worth every bit of your time and energy. If you put in the work up front, you'll find that your village will serve as a valuable resource for companionship, referrals and recommendations, favor swapping, and a thousand other things. Every slice of your pie will see improvement. When emergencies arise, the support provided by a village allows you to minimize the impact on your career. Meanwhile, with all the time you'll save by having proper child and home care in place, you'll be able to put that much more of yourself into other important slices of your pie, such as your health, your social life, and your community.

You can do a lot on your own, but you can do so much more when you have people backing you up. Take care of your village, and your village will take care of you.

PART III

SLICES

CHAPTER EIGHT

CAREER

Passion and persistence are what matter.

— Diane von Furstenberg

It is easy to think of your career as something driven by luck or fate or your boss or some other uncontrollable force, but the truth is that you are the baker here: you are the one with the mixing bowl and the ingredients and you need to create your own recipe for this slice of your pie. Managing your career as a working parent requires that you rise to the occasion, get in the zone, and perform at your best. This doesn't mean you have to be performing on a tightrope, but it does mean that you have to be deliberate about how you navigate your career.

It was Greek scientist Archimedes who first advanced the concept of using a lever to move objects that otherwise would have been far too heavy to lift. Likewise, to navigate your career as one of the busiest women on the planet, you need to identify and use your professional levers. Here are the top 12 levers that will maximize your career potential. Recall Estée Lauder's quote at the beginning of chapter 5. "I didn't get there by wishing for it . . . but by *working* for it!"

Seek Out Sponsors

According to Sylvia Ann Hewlett's Center for Talent Innovation, a New York–based think tank, women don't wallow in subpar careers because they lack ambition, skills, or experience, but because they lack a senior-level champion who will advocate for their raise or promotion. So how do you get someone to champion you? You shouldn't directly ask a higher-up; author Sheryl Sandberg cautions against this approach in her book *Lean In: Women, Work, and the Will to Lead,* and Hewlett echoes her sentiments. But there are ways to get a senior colleague to become more than a mentor. It starts with offering to help your desired advocate with a project or asking for a meeting in which you can solicit advice about your career goals.

When I served as an assistant at Ted Turner's film studio in Century City, Scott Sassa, then Ted's right-hand man, flew in to hold a town hall meeting with the entire staff. I intentionally secured a front row seat and followed Scott out of the auditorium when he was done. "Mr. Sassa, hi!" I said. "I am an assistant in the film department and would love some career advice. Do you have time to sit with me for 10 minutes while you're in town?" He agreed, and when we got together, I told him what I loved about the work I was doing and peppered him with questions on what my next move should be. He seemed to appreciate the fearless nature of my slightly immature yet enthusiastic approach and my genuine interest in his counsel. From that day on, Scott became not just a trusted career mentor but also a sponsor. Again and again, he offered me opportunities and counseled me as I fielded job offers from others and navigated my career.

As you dream about your future career, remember that it all starts with people. Who do you want to work for or with? Who will help boost your career while still respecting your personal life? Identify these leaders and approach them. Over the years I have found that luminaries and titans of industry get approached far less than you'd think, and if you take time to think carefully about what to say when first making contact, you will most often get the response you want. Women I have interviewed, from designer Liz Lange to Laurel Richie, former president of the Women's National Basketball Association, all tell me they respond to cold contacts. If you are already in a company, chances are even greater that a senior leader will be willing to talk to you and build a relationship with you.

Many women I meet are afraid to stand out; they feel most comfortable safely "blending in." Here's the problem: Avoid standing out, and you ensure that you'll never *be* a stand out. You'll never distinguish yourself from your peers, and bosses will likely overlook you for promotions or other opportunities. If you stand out through hard work, a proactive nature, creativity, and an "always learning" mentality, you can't help but ascend.

Steer Clear of Bad Bosses, Not Bad Industries

A woman I know proudly told me about an encounter she recently had with her 16-year-old daughter. The teenager had told her mom that she wanted to be in the restaurant business; the mom responded by saying that it would be impossible to work in the restaurant industry and have a family, so her daughter should choose another field. As she recounted the story to me, this mother was certain that I would love the advice she had given. I was startled and overcome with frustration. This woman's daughter had shared a dream and her mother had immediately squashed it. If her son had come to her with a similar dream, would the advice have been the same? Not a chance.

Plus, this advice was dead wrong. From a lifestyle perspective, "good" and "bad" industries don't exist. You could work in the most "family friendly" field in the world and have a boss with no personal life who expects you to work like he or she does. Or you could work in a field with notoriously tough hours and still carve out a niche for yourself, enjoying more time with your family.

But this woman wasn't simply guilty of being wrong. She was guilty of bruising and likely crushing her daughter's dream. As someone who spends my career thinking about work/life integration, I am not in the business of squashing dreams; my job is to tweak your lifestyle so you can pursue *all* of your dreams without guilt or hesitation. Why relegate a child (or any woman!) to the sidelines before she even plays in the game? Where there's a will to pursue a career in a given field, there is almost always a way.

Just ask finance executive Andria Weil. Although she had chosen a traditionally male industry to work in, she learned to focus on finding the right men to work for, those who didn't see baby making as an obstacle. As she recalls, "Many of them only cared about my intellect and never doubted my capabilities, even when I was very pregnant with my third child." Andria also knew how important it was to find a company that would respect her personal life. When she attended business school, she made the conscious decision to interview for jobs while she was noticeably pregnant with her second child. Andria felt that if a company didn't want to hire a mom, then she would rather find out at the start. Some companies she targeted had absolutely no desire to continue the conversation once they saw her pregnant belly, but the consulting firm McKinsey did. Executives there openly talked about Andria's decision to work and be a mom and how she could pull it off at their organization. It required some negotiation, but Andria and the company both wanted her to succeed. And succeed she did.

Ace the Job Interview

Lisa, a public relations veteran and mom of two, asked me for advice on how she should handle an upcoming slew of job interviews. Should she tell potential employers in advance that she was hoping to work one or two days a week from home? I advised against it. Far better, I thought, to secure the opportunity first and then attempt to meld it to her specifications. Once a prospective employer fell for her, they would probably be more willing to bend so she would take the job and thrive in it. But if she asked for concessions before having been offered the opportunity, the employer would compare her to other candidates who didn't make comparable requests. She would be a noncandidate from the very beginning.

What if you've already broached a request related to work/life balance? Don't worry—it's possible to land that job anyway. Laura Dicterow worked for 18 years as a development manager at the Humane Society of America before leaving her job to have a baby. Five years later, with her only child in first grade, she was itching to return, but she didn't know how to take the first step. Laura looked online to see what was out there and found a job opening that seemed perfect: development manager at a nonprofit called Farm Sanctuary. Laura really wanted to work from home two days a week, so before formally applying, she wrote an e-mail asking if that would be a possibility. When she met with me one day later, I suggested she act as though she had never sent that first e-mail and instead, apply formally to the human resources department with her resume and professional cover letter. She did that and was called in for an interview the next day.

During the interview and others that followed it, nobody mentioned Laura's initial e-mail and she, likewise, said nothing about flexibility. She gained confidence as she proceeded through the interview process and was thrilled when they offered her a position. Only at that point did Laura inquire about flexibility: Could she work from home two days a week if she made all of her deliverables and did a great job? They agreed without hesitation. Months later when I checked in with Laura, she told me how much she loved her new position. She found her work more satisfying than ever, and she still had plenty of time to spend with her daughter.

Some employers aren't nearly as generous, and once you have the offer in hand, you can choose whether to take the position or not. But only once you receive an offer do you have that choice. When employers meet a job candidate who has taken time off to have kids, they typically fear that the candidate will start in the position, receive weeks or months of expensive training, and then quit because they can't readjust to the working world. When interviewing, it is your job to make their decision an easy one. Describe how much you love to work and explain that you are the hardest worker you know. It's hard not to hire a workhorse, so present yourself as one. This advice holds true whether you are returning to the workforce after taking time off, or just interviewing for a new position.

Adjust Your Time Horizon

If you have one or more children below the age of 5, ease up on yourself and realize that for many women, these are the "Maintenance Years," the time to sustain your career and keep your contacts warm. If you can come out of these five years with your network and your resume intact, you are a winner. Once your kids attend school full-time, you can return once again to "go for it" mode. The Maintenance Years involve hard-core manual labor at home, so don't pressure yourself to leapfrog five levels in your career (while also staying happy and healthy!). Some women do manage to pull this off, but if you choose to slow down, don't beat yourself up. Instead, celebrate the fact that you have sustained your career during an extra-challenging time in your life.

Morra Aarons-Mele, founder of the digital marketing agency Women Online, does not hide the FOMO (fear of missing out) she has felt as the mom of three small children. "I read about my peers whose businesses are growing amazingly and who are speaking all over the world and doing really exciting things, and I'm thinking: 'I am home changing diapers and wiping butts, and my business has really stayed about the same size for the past couple of years.'" Although the disparity burns a little, Morra tries to take a step back and put it in perspective. She still makes a great living, and she gets to spend two days a week with her kids. All things considered, she is thriving.

To make the most of your time during the Maintenance Years, find a work situation that suits you and stick with it. When her children were 2 and 6 years old, publishing executive Kathleen Schmidt left the corporate world to start her own firm. Her new office would be only five minutes from home, allowing her to be around her kids more. Kathleen acknowledges the career sacrifices this entailed, explaining that four years later when she wanted to return to the corporate world, it was far more difficult than she had anticipated. She eventually had to accept a lower-level job to get her foot back in the door. It was a wise move that led to her next position as a vice president and head of communications for a major publishing house.

In this position, she was required to make a different kind of sacrifice, commuting up to four hours a day so she and her family could live in a town with great schools. It was well worth it, she spent only nine months there before landing her current position as Associate Publisher of a major publishing house in New York, a job with more responsibiity, a bigger paycheck, and a relatively short 45 minute commute each way, shaving more than two hours off of her daily commute.

I love Kathleen's story not just because of her resourcefulness in landing her current position, but also because it shows how there is no perfect balance. At certain times in your life, one slice will take priority over another. A year later, another slice might take precedence. Staying adaptable and doing what it takes to meet your changing needs makes all the difference.

Be Fearless

When I was 18, I was the youngest intern at media giant Viacom, stuck with what appeared to be the least desirable job in human resources: flipping through hundreds of secretarial resumes and throwing away any that contained even a single typo. I lapped it up though; to me it felt like I was advising the president on selecting his next Supreme Court justice.

During the second week, my diligence got me noticed, and I was offered the opportunity to walk secretarial candidates to the testing room and administer their typing tests. I then walked them back to reception, where they would wait until my boss, a man named Paul, was ready to interview them. In the meantime, I would run to Paul's big, windowless office to share what I had observed about the candidates. "This one is very sweet and poised and confident." "This one said the oddest thing!" Paul loved it and encouraged me to share my opinions. During the third week, I was asked to sit with the big boss's secretary to help her decide which candidates to interview. There was no happier or more grateful intern on the planet.

When the fourth week hit, I heard rumblings about a company picnic. Viacom would bus us all out of the city to enjoy a barbecue, field day activities, a dance party, and tennis. I had heard that Viacom's CEO at the time, Frank Biondi, was an avid tennis player, and as a nationally ranked junior player myself (on my way to play my first year on the college team), I decided that I should see if Frank wanted to play against me at the company picnic. Blissfully naïve about office politics and hierarchy, I sent him a handwritten note via interoffice mail. (Remember those big yellow envelopes from the days before e-mail?) The letter highlighted my tennis ranking, explained that I was an intern, and invited him to play at the picnic.

A week later, I had all but forgotten about the letter when Paul's assistant, Sonya, raced into his office to find me. "Samantha!" she said, catching her breath. "Frank Biondi's secretary is on the phone for *you*! How do you know her?"

I darted to her desk to take the call. Mr. Biondi's secretary got straight to the point. "Mr. Biondi will meet you at 1:00 p.m. at the tennis courts on Wednesday."

Game on.

From that moment forward, the head of human resources, a woman named Colette whom I had never met before, glued herself to my side. She even sat with me on the bus to the picnic, presumably to ensure her spot at the tennis match. We played in front of hundreds of people. The next week Mr. Biondi was reportedly heckled at a Viacom board meeting for losing to an intern.

Even if you don't want to risk beating the company CEO in his or her favorite sport, you can absorb a bit from the fearless nature of my tennis challenge. I was ignorant of politics; I took a chance that felt risk-free. What if you could do the same today? What risks would you take? Whom would you approach? What position would you go for? I'm not suggesting that you ignore office politics, but we tend to use it as an excuse not to go for the raise or the promotion. It helps to ask yourself what you would do if politics were not a factor and then back into how to handle it given your goals.

When I put my *Experts' Guide* book series together, it required the same confidence it took to contact Frank Biondi. Each book was meant to be a CliffsNotes take on important life skills, featuring 100 chapters written by the top experts across a variety of fields. I cold-called hundreds of experts to ask them to write a chapter for the book. From Barbara Corcoran to Richard Branson, they said yes to writing a 500-word essay on their area of expertise, because of the confidence with which I approached them. Sure, I received more than one "no" along the way, but I tend to forget those. I knew rejection was part of the process. When you sit down in advance and anticipate how it'll feel when you get a no, it takes away some of the fear. As cliché as it sounds, "What's the worst thing that could happen?" is really one of the *best* questions to ask yourself.

From the very beginning of her career, designer Liz Lange had no fear. Liz pioneered stylish maternity wear at a time when nobody was interested in pregnant celebrities, let alone looking stylish when pregnant. If it weren't for her attitude, she would have never succeeded, and stylish maternity wear might never have been created. Most people are stunned to learn that the biggest success of Liz's career came from a cold call.

When Liz was already established, she wanted to grow her brand and felt that Target would be her ideal partner. But she didn't know anyone at the company. So what did she do? She picked up the phone and talked her way to someone who might help. Eventually, she found herself speaking with the right person. That conversation led to a successful partnership, which has now made Liz Lange the nation's number one maternity wear brand.

We tend to enter our careers fearlessly, only to lose that feeling once the responsibilities pile on. Describing her frustrations with her career in business development, Oklahoma-based Catina D'Achille traced it all back to fear: "Fear creeps in way too often and the fear of failure, the opinions of others, and the fear of the unknown handicap me too much. I yearn for thicker skin so I do not overanalyze every decision or response I make." To get thicker skin, it helps to realize that we are all imperfect and prone to mistakes. I like to suggest on my radio show that if you won't work on your fears for your own well-being, do it for your children's sake. They are, after all, watching your every move and looking to you as a role model.

FAULTY MATH

The Mistake: A couple will sit down and look at the lesser-earning spouse's income, comparing that with the annual cost of a nanny or day care. This comparison will lead them to conclude that the lesser-earning spouse should drop out of the workforce.

The Solution: Compare the lesser-earning spouse's future earnings (until age 75) to the cost of a nanny or day care *for the first five years* of baby's life. We now know that off-ramping for just a year can mean a loss of 18 percent of future earnings. This number jumps to 38 percent when women take three or more years off.[xx] So a correct calculation requires that you compare child-care costs to current *and* future earnings. This equation is compelling even without including such other important factors as satisfaction, fulfillment, the social impact, and the chance to serve as a role model to your children.

To ascend in your career, you have no choice but to replace at least some of your fear with the joy of possibility. Once again, you are the baker, and only you can make the ingredients work well together. Once you realize this, there is no limit to what you can achieve.

Get Social

Social media is an added tool in your kit regardless of your industry. If you are an attorney and building a social media following doesn't seem like it would enhance your career goals, then become a voyeur, using social media to follow your 40 favorite news outlets and thinkers. It's a huge time-saver—a one-stop shop for gathering your daily news. However, if you are among the 90 percent of women who *can* benefit from building a following or amassing industry contacts, then start using social media aggressively.

Let's say you're working for a big firm that specializes in naming companies, and you choose to take the entrepreneurial leap and start your own business in that space. Social media provides free marketing for you starting today. Hanging your own shingle has never been cheaper or easier. Make @NamingQueen your new Twitter and Instagram handle, start posting about names you love and links to your favorite industry articles, follow all of the industry players, and you are in business. If you are looking to be an etiquette expert, find a handle that screams your new expertise, like @Howtobehave, and get to work by following the industry leaders, offering up your advice, and creating a following.

On social media, expanding your network is as simple as following the top names in your industry or those you admire and interacting with them on Facebook, LinkedIn, Instagram, and Twitter. I will never forget the first time I interviewed banking executive Sallie Krawcheck for a corporate video series. She acted like we were old friends even though we had never met. Why? Because we had "met" on Twitter, interacting for two years prior to our face-to-face encounter.

The best part about social media for busy women is that it requires no face time and can be done on your own schedule. Once you learn it, you can do it during off hours, whether that's on the train home from work or between innings at your daughter's softball game.

Network Like a Pro

I love asking women if they're good at networking. If I pose the question to a room of 100 women, two or three hands will go up. I then ask another question: "How many of you are good at helping other people?" Now there are 100 hands.

From now on, let's look at "networking" as just a fancy word for "helping." When you help people, it comes back to you many times over. Helping is the basis for *all* networking. Of course, you shouldn't help a person who expects or demands help or a certain level of gratitude in return. Networking is a numbers game, but it is *not* one-for-one reciprocation. The more you help, the more help you receive, but not necessarily from the same people you helped.

If you aren't a natural networker, you might doubt whether chances to help really arise that often. But they do! There is no better and easier way to give than to open up your list of contacts. The more free-flowing you are with introductions, the more successful and satisfied you will be. What could be better than introducing two people who do a business deal, or write a book together, or form a carpool? Whatever the connection is, when you make it, magic happens.

Let's say your neighbor is looking for someone to help with her will. You have a lawyer friend who works at a big firm with a trust and estates department. What do you do? *Make an intro.* Or perhaps a mom friend at school is a real estate broker, and you have a friend looking to sell her home. Once again, *make an intro.* Or let's say your friend is looking to build her party planning business. Another friend's brother is a caterer. Yet again, *make an intro.*

Sallie Krawcheck regards networking as the number one unwritten rule of business success. "One of the reasons men begin to pass women in their mid-thirties," she writes, "isn't that they are better at their jobs; it is that they have better networks." Thanks to these networks, men don't merely *know* more people, they gain more access to job opportunities. As Sallie notes, "Your next business opportunity is more likely to come from a loose connection than a close connection."

No matter what role you perform, networking makes you more valuable to your company and your colleagues. People used to stay with the same company for 30 or 40 years before retiring, but these days, company hopping is rampant. Every time a colleague leaves your company, an opportunity opens for you to gain a new contact at another company. Keep in touch with your old colleagues by meeting for lunch or coffee. Those old college friends? Keep in touch with them too. Your neighbor who happens to be in your field? Keep in touch. The wider your network, the more valuable you are to your employer and the greater your chances of hearing about new opportunities.

Learn Your Industry

As a busy woman, you are not going to win the face time game—and I suggest you don't even try, because that would be a battle you don't want to win—so you need to seek out other ways to distinguish yourself. As with most things, knowledge is power. The more industry expertise you can gain, the more valuable you become.

I began my media career as an assistant at the Hollywood talent agency CAA (Creative Artists Agency). From the moment I stepped into the agency's noisy, testosterone-filled halls, I realized that my value would largely hinge on the names I knew. I didn't need to personally know Barry Diller or Sherry Lansing, but I needed to know who they were. I needed to know the names of the top directors, actors, screenwriters, development executives, and producers. If I did, I could weasel my way into almost any conversation that mattered. I succeeded in that first job because I made it my business to meet as many people in the industry as possible and to voraciously read the trade publications each morning.

Years later, when I transitioned to the tech publishing world, I maintained my Hollywood knowledge by continuing to read all that I could. This practice paid off a couple of years later, when I wanted to reenter the world of film and television. I returned seamlessly, talking the talk and behaving as though I had never left. The old saying that knowledge is power holds true, especially in the workplace. The more you know about your industry and area of expertise, the more valuable you become to your employers and your colleagues.

Stay Razor-Focused

When Maria Seidman was pregnant with her second child, she participated in a call with her company's cofounder *on her due date*. "I started having contractions," Seidman remembers, "but we were getting so much done that I didn't say anything. I just quietly timed them. When the clock struck 1:00 a.m., he said he had to go to sleep and I wished him good-night. Then I called my doctor to tell her I was coming in because my contractions were just a few minutes apart."

Maria wasn't hiding her labor from her colleague; she simply knew that her time was limited and she didn't want to waste it. While this example might sound extreme, this kind of discipline is critically important. If you feel under the weather and you're on the phone with a client that you seldom talk to, isn't it better to not mention your flu symptoms? If you spend five minutes of the call talking about your illness, you leave less time for real work, and your client hangs up with a lasting image of you sick in bed. Nobody wins. Mothering is tough, but know when to share it—and when not to.

PR Yourself

Men are typically far better at singing their own praises than women, while most women find it easier to compliment others. To reach your potential, you need to do the most you can to promote yourself. You can't afford to rely on others to praise your strengths and talk about your accomplishments—it needs to come from *you*.

Know and appreciate your achievements, whether it's exceeding sales goals by 25 percent, getting promoted twice in three years, or landing a new client. When people ask how your job is going, have nuggets ready to share with them, such as, "I worked really hard this year, as did my team, and we exceeded our sales goals by 25 percent." People are far too busy to "discover" your accomplishments, so it is up to you to share them. Staying with the facts or stats or quoting others singing your praises is preferable to subjectively saying, "I am awesome at sales." This helps you avoid crossing the line to bragging.

The compliment is the cousin of this issue. When you receive a compliment, the only appropriate reaction is to say thank you. When you are told your coat is lovely and you respond with, "This beat-up old thing? I bought it at a thrift store 10 years ago," you are inadvertently criticizing the person's taste. Similarly, when you are told you did a great job at work and you say, "Oh it was nothing," you are putting the compliment giver in an uncomfortable spot. Part of living the Pie Life is making your value known and being efficient with your time. In the case of compliments and singing your own praises, it pays to master these skills so that you move faster and more effectively through your career.

Shine Through Your Attitude

We now know that people heal faster, attract romantic partners easier, and live longer if they maintain a positive attitude. If you don't think positive, start doing it—fast. A positive attitude will take you far in the corporate world, making it easier to thrive and to bounce back from inevitable setbacks.

When Sallie Krawcheck was fired from Bank of America, it made the front page of the *Wall Street Journal*. Her reaction speaks volumes. On day one after her firing, she drank wine. On the second day, she "received" e-mails and notes from old friends and colleagues. On the third day, she acted, calling every board member of the company that fired her to thank them, express what an honor it was to work for the company, and ask how she might improve her performance for next time.

Imagine you are a hiring manager. If you need to let go of one employee, would it be Debbie Downer or Ursula Upper? If you can only promote one of two employees and they both have equal strengths, which one does the promotion go to?

To project a positive attitude at the office, pay attention to these three things:

React emotionally. Yes, there are times to get emotional at work. Is there anything worse than a person who reacts to great news with barely a flicker of light? While you shouldn't be a puddle of emotions, it is okay and often helpful to show your happiness at appropriate times. When your team reaches its sales goal or a colleague shares an accomplishment, be the first one to celebrate with genuine well-wishes.

Don't huff and puff. Never utter the words "that is not my job" or muddle resentfully through a task that you deem beneath you. Be the team player who proactively asks what the greatest challenge is and how you can help solve it.

Stay out of the fray. It can be tempting to engage in office gossip, but resist the urge. So much good comes from being the one who smiles at the office and is kind to everyone. Once you become known for staying out of back talk, you will thankfully lose your invitation to the gossip circle. Good thing: this is one party you should be happy to skip.

Know When to Say Good-Bye

A corporate environment can be an intoxicating place. You have work friends, perks, office supplies, sales incentive trips, and generous vacation policies all at your fingertips. In addition, you know all the rules and personalities and how to navigate them. So you feel comfortable. Maybe too comfortable. If you have kids, you might feel more reluctant to change jobs, even when you know deep down that you should. After all, the unknown seems far riskier than the status quo when you feel stretched and stressed at home.

Nobody but you can navigate your career. Kristal Bergfield, who runs customer service for a start-up, recalls staying at American Express years longer than she had intended. Initially she found herself stuck because she couldn't figure out where she wanted to go next. Once the financial crisis hit, she continued to stay out of fear. "Being at a company long term is almost like a marriage," she reflects. "You might know it's over, but it takes a while to extricate yourself."

If you are feeling stuck, ask yourself what you would say to your best friend or your adult child if she found herself in the same circumstances as you. Would you advise her to languish on in a job in which she has stopped learning or growing? Would you tell her to stay put even though the prospects for advancement have dried up? Certainly not. So it's time to give yourself the same advice. Know when to say good-bye. And if that time has arrived, do it.

Speed Up the On Ramp

Whether it's four hours a week or full-time, it pays to keep working (even when your kids are small!). Always keep your foot in the door, because you never know when you'll need it to open. Only 40 percent of women who want to return to full-time work after off-ramping actually do.[18]

When our daughter Ruby was three and we had just moved to Los Angeles, I took her to a soccer class. I was surrounded by vibrant moms, including a former attorney, a former magazine editor, and a former marketing executive. They had each taken between five and seven years off to raise their kids, and each expressed a desire to get back into the workforce. Unfortunately, each felt powerless to do so. The marketing executive complained that her contacts had run cold. The magazine editor lamented that when she last worked, the Internet wasn't around; she saw herself as a dinosaur. The attorney explained that she hadn't kept up with her specific field, which had changed considerably.

If you have already left the workforce completely, here are six ways to up your game as you get back in:

Get out of preschool. When introducing yourself, always use your first and last name no matter the setting. There are too many Jennifers out there for you to be memorable without two names. You were "Jenny" in preschool. Now you're "Jenny Miller."

Tell your story. When asked what you do at a dinner party or at the playground, always give your history. "I spent 10 years in marketing and now I am home for a couple of years with the kids" is a far better answer than "Oh, I'm at home with the kids." The first answer begins a conversation; the second one ends it.

Keep in smart *touch*. When keeping in touch with old colleagues, don't just share baby photos through Instagram. Instead, send an industry-related article with a note saying that it "made me think of you."

Don't be a dinosaur. I am always amazed by the number of women who brag about not knowing what Twitter is or about being off Facebook. Foregoing social media is the fastest way to become irrelevant. It ages you on the inside just as sitting in the sun ages you on the outside.

Make yourself the easy hire. When you have a gap in your resume, your interviewer will have a hard time pitching you internally. Make her job a bit easier by telling her how passionate you are about the field and how hard you work.

Describing the Maintenance Years, journalist Lisa Belkin observes: "This period of intensity where you are doing everything at once and firing on cylinders you don't have—we tend to think that this lasts forever. What I have figured out is that it is a concentrated period in a lifetime." Devon Pike, president of Givenchy USA and mom of a young daughter, also says she would tell her younger self not to take the early years of motherhood—or in fact any time in her life—so seriously. "I spent a lot of time trying to evaluate every little piece of the opportunity and do every piece perfectly. It had to be exactly the right moment and I had to have accomplished exactly this much to be able to be ready to meet the guy or to be ready to be a mother and actually, it is never the right moment."

Your career is long, and you hopefully will be physically capable of working until at least age 80. Though your career slice will contract and expand over the years, you never want to let it disappear completely. Don't make short-term decisions like staying home for two years while your child is an infant, especially if that means giving up your long-term career path. It pays both figuratively and literally to consider your future dreams and to realize that this slice will require constant changes to its recipe. Check in often with yourself to see if your current recipe is as delicious as it could be. If it isn't, be resourceful and proactive about adding the optimal ingredients.

CHAPTER NINE

CHILDREN

Childhood is a short season.

— Helen Hayes

The goal of being a great parent is so enormous that it could easily eclipse every-thing else in your life. I encounter parents every day who feel they can't advance their other slices because this one piece of the pie requires constant attention.

Some parents struggle each day with a multitude of conflicting pick-ups and drop-offs and logistics that need to happen while they are at work. Others battle their children on a daily basis over issues like homework or taking too long to put on shoes in the morning. This, on top of the sleep deprivation, can wear anyone down. In the baby years and beyond, the exhaustion and the end-less needs of child rearing—from keeping up with the wardrobes of fast-growing children to making doctors' appointments and setting playdates and packing lunches and backpacks, all while getting your job done—becomes a seemingly impossible and almost laughable set of responsibilities. Still others have a child with serious emotional or physical problems that require constant attention. Whatever the case, when one of the most important slices of your pie isn't work-ing the way you had envisioned, it can consume your energy and crush your spirit, leaving you with anything but a thriving life.

Here's the good news: I have a system that will make your parenting far more efficient and enjoyable. It's called "intentional parenting" and I think you'll find it will help you excel as a parent and make parenting decisions easier. Intentional parenting is centered on building a strong, positive family culture and sense of identity; once you establish this, you will see your family thrive. If you can create this culture, it will make your parenting easier for years to come and it will help your kids develop a foundation of inner confidence and pride in their family. Of course, this also means that the other slices of your pie will benefit too because your parenting will be more manageable and less likely to overwhelm the other slices.

This approach came from a combination of my own experience working with countless women and realizing that in order to lead a productive daily life, success in building a family culture and identity is critical. What I have included here are the quickest fixes that have the highest impact; these are adjustments to some of the biggest challenges that can absorb most of your time and create the most friction. Once you incorporate these changes into your life, you'll be able to make the most of the time you have for your parenting piece of pie.

Perhaps the best aspect of intentional parenting is its efficiency. If your career or another large slice of your pie commands much of your attention, you don't have unlimited time to spend with your kids. You have to be extremely careful about how you use the time you *do* have. Intentional parenting allows you to make the most of every week, every day, every hour, even every minute, so that you have space in your life for those other important slices. Intentional parenting achieves this because as time passes, the family culture you're building starts to do much of the work, reducing friction in your home and easing your parenting burden. We want mornings before our kids walk out the door to feel like a launch pad, not a battlefield. Evening dinners should be a time to feel connected rather than sources of guilt. And weekends should be as relaxing as possible, not taxing.

Like any family, everyday home life isn't always pretty. In our family, we have tears, but we have far more laughs; we have fights, but we have far more peace; we have low points but more often high ones. I am certain that the hard work we have put into our parenting has paid off. Our kids are good listeners, they respect our rules, and they are kind, confident people. My husband and I are both aware that our role as parents never ends; who they are today does not guarantee who they will be tomorrow, so we are constantly working on it. Like us, you don't have the excess time in your life that reactive parenting requires, so by parenting intentionally, you will be proactively making your life easier.

As we discussed in other chapters, try incorporating a few of these strategies to start, and then come back later to add in others. Just as it is never too late to start a new fitness program, it is never too late to create a strong family culture that lets you whip your parenting slice into shape. The time is always right to become an intentional parent. Parenting is a long roller coaster. Hop on and I will show you how to make the ride a little smoother with these intentional parenting strategies.

1. Outline the Rules

Kids crave consistency and structure. One of the most important ways that a strong family culture reduces tension is by affirming clear family rules and an expectation that we all live by them. (And that's important: to make these rules stick, we parents must live by them too.) By using the phrase "our family" when outlining rules and even general approaches to life, they become more of a family ideology rather than some oppressive and opaque doctrine your kids are asked to follow. Using "our family" when we talk about a rule makes it so that we rarely get to a point where discipline is needed, and using it to describe pleasures and preferences helps define our family culture.

The mantra of "our family" is an extremely basic but critically important technique. If my four-year-old child hits me on the leg, I will say, "Our family doesn't hit." If I want to make sure my child doesn't chew gum, I say, "Our family doesn't chew gum." But I'm not the only one who's saying "Our family." I will never forget the time I escorted my daughter Ella to a birthday party for her classmate who had just turned five. The goody bags were distributed mid-party, and Ella ran up to me with the bag in one hand and her other hand tightly closed. She opened her fingers to reveal nail polish and lip balm. As she handed it to me, she said, "Mom, here. In our family, kids don't wear makeup." Score! And today, when our 25-year-old cousin comes for dinner and starts texting, Ella and Ruby are the ones who tell her that "our family" doesn't use phones at the table. Can you say *amazing*?

Do you feel resistant to putting "our family" into action? I was at first. I was not only worried that we would offend other parents, but that we were going to make our own kids resent "our family" for its abundant and clear rules. Years later, Mitch and I look back and agree that not only has this strategy worked, but it has become one of our most reliable tools.

This mantra works in part because it meshes together some pretty strict rules with the enjoyable, fun parts of being a family—as a result, it doesn't feel oppressive. We probably have more rules than other families, but we reinforce them with accolades for what our kids are doing right versus punishment for what they are doing wrong. We don't simply say, "In our family, we don't use makeup." We also say, "Our family listens to one another," "Our family comforts each other when we are sad," "Our family loves to spend time together," "Our family loves to dress alike on Halloween . . ."

Another reason the "our family" mantra works is that we give our kids a hand in defining what "our family" is and does. The framework for defining "our family" is what we call the "Family Constitution." Just as our country has a constitution, so, too, does your family deserve one. Here's how it works: You all sit down for a fun family meeting (bring treats!), and every member of speaking age can contribute things that they would like to add to the constitution. These could include ideas like: "We show up on time for each other," "If we hear someone talking about our sibling, we always stand up for one another rather than joining in," "No violence," "We cheer each other on at sporting events or school whenever possible," "We are inclusive," "We don't go to bed angry with each other," "We say 'I love you' before going to sleep," or "We hold hands on the airplane before takeoff."

The Family Constitution is an ever-evolving document that you rewrite each year. Your kids will feel ownership over your version of "our family" because they helped write the rules. This almost instantly reduces conflict. When you tell your son that he isn't allowed to play with toy guns because that's not what we do in "our family," he won't see it as an arbitrary and unpleasant rule that you as a parent just dreamed up. He'll see it instead as an unpleasant rule that is part of something bigger and wonderful that *he* helped create.

2. Rely on Rituals

As a working mom wanting to make the time you have with your kids as significant as possible, rituals are your best friend. This is not about face time as much as it is about fun time. You don't have endless time at home, and this is one key way to make the most of it. Rituals are the most high-value additions to your life and add enormously to a strong family unit.

Our family has instituted a Friday family movie night, and we all look forward to it. When we moved to California, we started a neighborhood Halloween party, inviting all the kids on the block. As I shared earlier, our Sunday dinners, which include a new family each week, have also become a ritual. We also celebrate national food holidays, a surefire way to give you the "fun parent" title. Look up the days online, pick five that you like, and add them to your calendar. Take your kids to the city's best donut shop on National Donut Day (first Friday of June), or bake a pie on National Apple Pie Day (May 13). You can't go wrong. It's not just because our kids gets a delicious donut or slice of homemade pie, but it's also a quirky ritual we look forward to that makes our family unique.

Rituals can be as simple as trying a new kind of lasagna every Thursday night, having Taco Tuesday nights, or celebrating the seasons together. Mark the arrival of autumn by making homemade pumpkin decorations and pasting them on the front door. Launch your summer with an official family trip to the beach. Do broccoli lasagna one week and Mexican lasagna the next and a make-your-own taco bar every Tuesday. In my experience, once you do a ritual three times, it turns into a tradition—and nothing bonds a family for life like traditions.

3. Parent to Type

When I was in my twenties, I worked for two female bosses. Although I had no children at the time and didn't even have kids on my mind, I still remember the dramatically different approach each boss took to parenting. Stacey would toss her new baby up in the air, gaze into the child's eyes, beaming, and say, "Who are you going to be?" And then there was Amy. She was married and didn't yet have kids, but she already knew everything about them. Their names, how she was going to dress them, which activities they would do. She had it all planned out.

Before having kids, I thought a lot about the contrast between these two strong women. I admired them both professionally, but when it came to which of them I wanted to emulate when I was a parent, the choice was clear. Amy was projecting her desires onto her child, setting herself up for inevitable conflict, disappointment, and heartache—not to mention confining her child to a preconceived box. Stacey had given her child a gift from infancy: the opportunity to be herself.

4. Inspire Their Potential

I grew up with parents who said "I love you" every single day. Saying "I love you" isn't just a way to express an emotion; it helps create a safe, warm family culture. As moral development expert Michele Borba explains, "'I love you' plants the most important message. Our kids need to develop those critical beliefs that say 'I'm a worthwhile person.' Our words become their inner dialogue."

Beyond "I love you," what else do kids need to hear constantly? When I used to interview successful and famous people for my Internet talk show *Obsessed TV*, 98 percent of interviewees had one thing in common: their parents made them believe they could be anything. Whether it was NBC's Al Roker, whose father drove a bus, or candy entrepreneur Dylan Lauren, daughter of famous father Ralph, each grew up hearing that the sky was the limit, and that if they worked hard they could achieve anything. I researched this further and found that this commonality is indeed shared by most of the world's most extraordinary people, from inventor Thomas Edison to Supreme Court justice Sonia Sotomayor. So share this message with your own kids: "I can do anything, I can achieve anything. I can be and become anything."

5. Improve Your Home

I remember when we first bought our house and I looked around at the family room dreaming of what it could be and how we would live in it. We didn't want to spend a lot of money on restructuring our new home because it was in good enough shape when we bought it and we wanted to use our budget for new furniture. The only structural change we made was to remove two pillars that separated the kitchen from the family room. We wanted an open floor plan, one where we could be cooking and the kids could be playing together in one big room.

The design of your home is no trivial thing; it determines a great deal about how your family functions. One of our biggest decisions was whether or not to put a TV in the family room; we opted not to. We've since made so many memories sitting around the kitchen table and in our living room, playing with

THE INTENTIONAL HOME EXERCISE

If you are single with young kids, try doing this exercise on your own. If you have a partner and kids ages 10 or over, do the exercise together. If you are coupled with young children, do it with your partner. Compare your answers, discuss them, and settle on qualities you agree on.

A. I want my home to feel _____, _____, and _____. (Choose three adjectives.)

B. I want to have _____, _____, and _____ in my home. (Choose three nouns. For example, you might want your home to be the gathering spot for the kids on the block. You might want it to be a peaceful sanctuary just for your family. You might want it to be neat and formal. So you would fill in the blank with "kids," "peace," or "order.")

C. Our home should be the kind of place where you walk in and _____. (For example, "feel calm," "get a warm feeling," "know that you are welcome," etc.)

D. How we behave in our home should reflect our family's values. Behaviors that reflect our values include _____, _____, and _____. (For example, "talking respectfully to one another," "showing one another affection," "listening before we assume," and so on.)

Legos or doing puzzles, enjoying time that inevitably would have been gobbled up by the television had we added one. This allowed us to make TV more of a special thing—Friday night movies, for example—while dulling the expectation that the kids could watch every night.

When designing your home's interior, make it as user-friendly as possible for the kids. Encourage their independence by putting their cups and plates within easy reach so they can help themselves. Do this with their toys and clothing too. We live in a world where 10-year-olds can make films and become chess prodigies; ours can at least learn the basics of daily life. The more you can encourage your kids to be independent, the more confident they will be, and the more helpful as well.

Make *how* you live in your home as intentional as the décor as well. In particular, minimize the stress and create a harmonious home that is a respite for your children and for you. As worried as you are about finances, your cat's injury, your angry client, and what you'll scrape together for dinner, take a breath and focus on the big picture for the sake of your innocent child. Exposure to an anxious parent leads children to develop anxiety themselves,[19] so making your home a source of peace is every bit as important as setting up a quiet spot to do homework. As actress Susan Yeagley reflects, "My husband and I are both actors, so we are used to unpredictability and changing schedules. Perhaps that's why we try to keep our home the opposite." In an uncertain world, your job is to make your home as solid, safe, loving, and peaceful as possible.

6. Control What You Can

When my oldest, Ella, was born, we realized that at least for a couple of years, we would entirely control the world around her, including what she heard, saw, felt, smelled, and tasted. We had a chance to make sure she got the best possible start—that her interactions with the world would all be wholesome and healthy. This understanding affected many decisions we made for her concerning her media habits, what she ate, whom she saw and when, what music she heard, and so on.

Kids are not born *wanting* chicken fingers, French fries, or macaroni and cheese. They are just as likely to crave lentils if you make it one of the first foods they eat and serve it consistently. Same goes for sweets, which is why when it came time for Ella's first birthday and people asked us what kind of cake we would be getting her, we were confused. Cake? Why would our one-year-old (who didn't yet have siblings to corrupt her palate) need a cake loaded with sugar? Instead, we invented a cantaloupe "cake." Ella's favorite food was cantaloupe so when she turned one, we cut a cantaloupe in half, carved out some pieces, and allowed her to dig in with her fingers. She was in heaven.

To this day, Ella is still the best eater in our family. As a three-year-old, she would proudly declare that her favorite foods were artichokes and capers. When our next daughter, Ruby, started eating solid foods, Ella was already 2 and had developed a taste for sweets. So naturally, Ruby was exposed to them at a far younger age because of her sister. I can no longer get away with serving cantaloupe cakes, but we still do our best to minimize the sugar for all three kids. For each child, what you can control will vary depending on an array of circumstances, including the presence of siblings, where you're living, the family's income, any health issues affecting the child, and so on. Don't worry about being the perfect parent. Just control as much as you can for as long as you can.

7. Inspire a Healthy Body Image

This is a tricky area for parents, and you will want to focus on it early to avoid giant problems down the road. It is essential that we inspire our kids to grow up loving their bodies. I have three children with three different body types, and my primary goal as a parent as far as their bodies are concerned is to raise them to love their bodies no matter what their shape or size. This is one of those areas that might seem insignificant when your kids are young, but you cannot afford to put this issue off. From other parents to television programs to advertising spreads and store windows, there is so much bad body image propaganda floating by your kids' eyes at a young age, and the more you are intentional about confronting this now, the more pain and time you will save later.

I know firsthand how important it is to send the right message about body image. During college, I lived with a severely bulimic roommate and, even before then, I served as an eating disorder counselor for a 24-hour student hotline. I've also dealt with fluctuations in my own weight over the years. As a child athlete, I never had to think about working out because my intense tennis schedule kept me fit. When I stopped playing, I gained 30 pounds, but I barely noticed thanks to all the confidence in my body I'd built up since childhood. It also helped that I had always seen my body as a source of athletic strength rather than beauty. I never dieted, and to this day I have yet to do so—a practice that has contributed to my healthy metabolism.

Today Mitch jokes that when I return for my college reunions, we walk into a recurring episode of *The Biggest Loser*. I have seen former classmates tear up when they see me, so thrilled to see I lost the weight they remember me having. I was heavy for only two years, but that image of me is seared in their memories. Not in mine. For this, I give my parents a ton of credit. They consistently told me that I was beautiful no matter what my weight, and they never said a word when I put on those 30 pounds.

I've come away from this experience wanting three things for my children pertaining to their bodies. First, I want them to see their bodies as sources of strength, not beauty. Secondly, I want them to love their bodies no matter the size. And third, I want them to never diet. If you can achieve these three goals, you have raised a kid with a healthy body image, and doing this now will save you tons of time and heartache down the road.

So how do you do it? When Ella was born, I made two rules for myself when it came to getting dressed: I would never have a wardrobe crisis in front of her, and I would always stick with the first thing I put on. This meant that Ella never saw me furiously yank off outfit after outfit in search of the perfect one. It didn't matter if I dreaded wearing the unflattering pants all day. As soon as I was wearing them, I told myself I was committed. Picking out the outfit the night before was extra insurance—I had taken the extra step to make my morning efficient, yet another reason not to turn back. No accident, then, that to date, my eight- and ten-year-old daughters have never had any clothing-related meltdowns or concerns. Will they ever be interested in clothing? Probably. I know I am. But as they enter their tween years, they have yet to focus on what they are wearing and their looks.

I want you to take this a step further, though, because it isn't enough to simply avoid complaining about your body once you have kids; you also must make every effort to show your kids that you *love* your body. This means when your child affectionately pushes your tummy and says, "Do you have a baby in there?" (even when you don't!), you say, "I love my belly." In general, one of your jobs as a parent is to *not* pass on your insecurities to your kids. At times, this can feel excruciating to pull off, but it's absolutely worth it. In time, all of the body love that you display for your kids will help you actually love your body more.

When Ruby was four, I took her to the beach with her friend and her friend's mom. The girls were running in and out of the ocean giggling as the water tickled their toes. The mom turned to me and pointed to a woman nearby whom I hadn't noticed and said, "I would kill for that body."

"Shhh," I exclaimed. "The girls are listening."

"Don't worry. They don't understand."

But they do. Our kids are always listening and learning, and these are the kinds of risks we can't afford to take.

Last year, we had a Fourth of July party and invited a bunch of families. A group of kids and parents were standing around the outdoor table when one mom hijacked the conversation with diet and body-hate talk. I changed the conversation and later took her aside to tell her that we don't have those kinds of conversations in my home. Did I lose a friend? In this case, no. But even if I had, it is my job to protect my kids as much as possible.

8. Lose the Labels

Children are growing and constantly changing inside and out. While it might be tempting to label our kids, it can cause them a lifetime of harm. The artistic one. The athletic one. The flirty one. The messy one. The mischievous one. At first, these labels seem fun and harmless, yet they tend to stick and constrain their development. As their natural inclinations bump up against our labels, our kids feel conflicted and lose confidence. Let's leave the labeling to food and wine. By holding back a little and fighting your inclination to label what we see, you can help your child reach his or her true, inner potential, whatever that may be.

When I enter a home and hear parents referring to one of their children as "the troublemaker" and another as "the lazy child," I can usually tell that they've been using that kind of language for years. Imagine if you were called "the careless one" at the office. Eventually you would lose confidence in your abilities and become more careless. Like adults, kids rise to or lower themselves to our expectations. So if you label your daughter "the troublemaker," she will assume

---

WHEN KIDS COMPARE

Kids naturally compare themselves to their friends: "Sadie is so lucky because she has sleepovers all the time," "Willa has the coolest train set," "Carter gets to stay up so much later than me." How you handle these comparisons will determine how often they come back at you. Here's a trick: Explain to your kids that life is not an *à la carte* Chinese menu. It's a package deal. If you had Chloe's toys, you would also have her parents and her home. If you went on Johnny's vacation, you would also have his siblings. You don't pick and choose the best of everyone else's life. This is a life philosophy and a great one to share with your kids.

---

that role and it will be hard for her to shake it. If you label her "the shy kid," you might have squashed her natural evolution into an extroverted teen.

Similar logic applies to how we talk about time. I call it the "bad day" trap. "Oh don't mind Hudson, he's having a bad day." When you label your child's day as "bad," you ensure that the rest of his day will be bad as well. The episode that prompted the label in the first place lingers on, when it should have quickly passed. If something unpleasant happens, you could avoid labeling it at all or refer to it as a "bad moment," because the next one could be glorious. It is impossible to inspire a positive outlook in your children with "bad day," "bad week," and "bad year" talk. So let's drop the labels for our kids and for these moments in time.

9. Yes, and . . .

In improvisational comedy, there is the golden rule of "Yes, and . . ." Amy Poehler's book, *Yes Please,* really schooled me on this one. If you're in the middle of a comedy sketch, you don't negate what the person before you said. Rather, you always agree and add something of value to the scene. Parents should do the same. If we respond with no, we close all the doors. When we say yes, we open the doors of possibility. Your child asks, "Can I have ice cream tonight?" You respond, "Well, we are having ice cream sundaes tomorrow night for dessert so you can definitely have it then!"

In a friction-free home, parents say yes whenever possible. Being a "no" parent almost by definition will create tension and constant frustration in your children. But saying yes doesn't mean always giving in. It means catching yourself before "no" becomes an instinct.

10. Don't Prematurely Age Your Child

I cringe when I hear parents boast, "My child is 5 going on 15." Why rush the aging process? The best thing that could happen to you is to have your 5-year-old act 5, your 11-year-old act 11, and your 15-year-old act 15. Our kids are only each age once, and each age carries its own gifts and wonders, so we might as well let them experience each. Keep in mind the goal: to raise healthy, independent kids and to do the best with the hours you have. When you age your children prematurely, you will find yourself battling a host of age-inappropriate behaviors—a first-grader chasing girls for kisses, or a third-grader begging for an Instagram account—and you will set yourselves up for potential future pitfalls that engulf an entire family in a host of problems.

One surefire way to help kids stick to age-appropriate behavior is to pay attention to their media diets. I have become completely dependent on resources like Common Sense Media, a website and app that reviews movies, books, and video games and labels them by age. The one area the site does not cover is gender, so I also use the website A Mighty Girl and my own independent research to curate my kids' media diet.

According to the Geena Davis Institute on Gender in Media, only 17 percent of speaking characters in family films are female. Richard Weissbourd, a child and family psychologist on the faculty of Harvard's Kennedy School of Government and its Graduate School of Education, explains that girls often limit their aspirations because "they see so few appealing characters in films who they identify with and want to be." Meanwhile, boys develop "narrow and impoverished" understandings of girls because "they see such a limited range of girls." As a mother, I want to make sure my kids get realistic and healthy ideas about gender—both their own and the other.

I've become extremely focused on curating my children's media diets (especially during these formative years of their lives) because of my experience working on Nickelodeon's preschool TV show *Blue's Clues*. I saw firsthand how great educational television for children really worked. Each episode was heavily researched in schools, and the content was perfectly tailored to young kids, with the host speaking directly to them on screen. By contrast, so many animated shows are not written with kids in mind. Producers and writers insert sarcastic, age-inappropriate jokes to keep parents entertained without regard for what's best for kids. Don't mistake animation for kids content. Choose wisely.

11. Curate the Company

You never want to spend so little time at home that you don't get to know the friends in your kids' lives. During the preschool years, you can subtly curate your children's friends by setting playdates with families whose values are similar to yours. As your children get older, help them make wise decisions about friends.

When my daughter was in second grade, she seemed to gravitate strongly toward a certain girl in the class, even though this girl had repeatedly brought her to tears. Apparently I had not done a good job of hiding my feelings, and one day Ella blurted out to me, "You hate Julia, don't you?"

"No," I responded, "I love any friend that makes you feel awesome inside. If you tell me that she makes you feel awesome inside, then I love her."

That has been my go-to line on friendship ever since. One of the greatest challenges of parenting is that you are constantly confronted with brand new situations that you need to react to on a dime. Having some magical techniques—tricks in your back pocket to rely on—reduces the number of times you will be caught empty handed. From now on, this line can be one of your back-pocket tricks too. When you parent with ease, your whole pie benefits.

12. Take Tears Seriously

You can't be there to kiss every scrape and scar, and this will end up making you a more effective parent. After all, there is no better protection against the dangers of helicopter parenting than working. Having a focus outside of your kids protects them from the hovering and anxious parenting associated with helicoptering. But when you are with your kids, you want to slow down enough to be present and show them that they are deserving of your spotlight. This means connecting with them emotionally, which brings me to the topic of tears.

I have two observations when it comes to tears. First, crying breeds crying. It's pure myth to think that if you leave a child alone to cry, you will show the child that tears don't work in getting their way, thereby prompting a more rational response next time. As numerous studies show, being nonresponsive to your child's crying can lead to more tears and a feeling of insecure attachment. If you don't respond that first time, the tears come harder next time, and harder still the time after that, until your child gets a response. It can also go the other way: if you don't respond over a period of time, your child will *never* cry because they internalize the idea that their feelings don't matter to the adults around them. This is the worst outcome of all because when they stifle their feelings, those feelings emerge destructively in other ways.

If your child is crying, there is always a reason. We tend to think that because our kids aren't crying about poverty in India or a massive fight with a loved one, they are getting worked up over tiny, silly things. But the things that upset them *are* big deals in their small worlds, and we must acknowledge that. The next time you are really sad, imagine someone you turn to for support ignoring your sadness or telling you that your feelings are silly. How much worse would that make you feel? That is exactly what we do when we let a child cry without emotionally comforting them.

"Yes," you might say, "but aren't I giving in by comforting my child?" No—empathy is wildly different from "giving in." By showing empathy, you're simply acknowledging your child's feelings, not expressing whether you agree with them, or whether you'll change your own decisions or behavior. By acknowledging how your child is feeling, you encourage him or her to label and understand their feelings going forward. Saying "I'm sorry you are so sad" or "You are really upset because you wanted the orange cup and not the red one" validates how your child feels, giving her a sense of security and protection. You don't *have* to give your child the orange cup; it's enough to simply acknowledge that she wanted it, that she is sad, and that she deserves a hug.

Family therapist Susan Stiffelman offers a technique here that works wonders. When your child is shedding big tears over something, eliciting "yeses" will help him feel understood. So for example, you ask, "You were hoping for the green cup?"

"Yes!" your child will say.

"The cup I gave you isn't the one you like best?"

"Yes!"

Once you get two or three yeses from your child, you will see an easing of his emotion because he feels validated. Later, you can offer a logical explanation like, "Jake has the green cup, so the only option is the blue one." But only after you have helped him through the storm of his emotions.

Similarly, when your child falls and you say "you're okay," you are teaching a child not to trust his own feelings or that his feelings don't matter. Contrary to what some people believe, this does not make your children tougher; it simply stifles their natural feelings and is the opposite of the empathetic reaction that they need from you in that moment.

13. Apologize in Their Presence

How do you teach children to take accountability for their behavior? The best way is to apologize to them or your partner or your friend when *you* do something wrong.

One morning when my husband was traveling and I was trying to get all three kids fed and dressed and to school on time, I lost it. Ruby and Bowen were ready to go, so I told Ella we would be in the car waiting for her while she put her shoes on. Two minutes later, there was still no sign of Ella, so I dashed into the house and found her dillydallying by the sneakers, with none on her feet. I did what I try so hard to avoid: I yelled, prompting her to cry.

This episode not only cost us time, but it shook her to the core. Seeing her so sad shook me too, and pretty soon we were both distraught. She was crying and telling me that I think she is a slow-moving person and that I hate her. She had interpreted my yelling as hatred. We got her sneakers on and returned to the car, but now we were really late *and* Ella was hysterically crying.

I challenged myself to use the seven-minute car ride to get this right. I began by asking: Did they remember that I had spoken at the University of Southern California the night before? They uttered a collective yes. "Well, last night there were a bunch of students who had done a case study—studying my business—and then I went to the class to hear them present their results and ask me questions. They told me about all of the things that were wrong with my brand. They thought I didn't reveal enough personal information in my speeches, which made me unapproachable."

As I continued to share the criticism I had heard, the kids were riveted and Ella's crying stopped. Then I said, "And you know, the next part of the presentation was telling me all of the things I was doing right, areas I was great in. But guess what? All I could hear was the bad stuff. And today when I was frustrated with Ella about her sneakers, she could only hear my frustration and missed all of the times this morning when I was hugging her, telling her how much she makes me laugh, or telling her how proud I was about the spelling test she had just aced."

The kids got the message: we tend to hear negative things before we hear the positive. By the time we arrived at school, Ella's tears had given way to a smile. We hugged and kissed and I apologized before she went into her classroom.

BlogHer founder Lisa Stone tells the story of being on a business trip in January 2011 and getting the call that every parent dreads. "One of the kids was in emotional free fall," she explains, "and I had to come home NOW. That wasn't a problem. What was a problem was the regret and guilt I had about the two years leading up to the crisis where I felt I had put the nagging issue of this child's needs on the same level of priority as my company's needs. Looking back, I would play this differently. And I've told the child so as well. Those mea culpas matter to me—and, I think, to them." The more honest you are with your children about your own shortcomings and mistakes, the more comfortable they will be communicating their own.

14. Turn Off the Tech

One of the best gifts you can give to your child is 90 minutes of focused time without technology each day. That means that even when you're dying to check your work e-mail at the dinner table because you're waiting for an answer from your boss, you stay focused and resist looking at your phone. The rewards are bountiful. As Katie Hood, mom of four and CEO of the One Love Foundation, explains, "My kids know that I love them above all else. When I am with them, I am fully engaged, frequently leaving my phone aside and focusing just on them—romping in the pool, jumping on the trampoline, walking them to school, shopping for back-to-school."

Turning off the technology for a period of time each day tells your kids that they are important to you and worthy of your full attention. This is the time that you can make up for not being the mom who is at pick-up every day. One hour of concentrated attention is better than 10 hours of distracted parenting. As Gayle King says, "When kids think you care, they care what you think." Use tech expert Carley Knobloch's "parking lot" rule. When you walk in the house, park your devices in a basket at the front door, or establish certain parking lot hours for your personal technology. This has the double bonus of serving as a great behavioral model for kids as they enter their teen years—they will need to park their devices too.

15. Pass on Your Strengths, Not Your Weaknesses

I grew up in New York City and am admittedly most comfortable indoors. Mitch is more of a mountain man, happiest when pitching a tent or on a hike. My outdoor phobias are countless, and when my first daughter was born, I was determined not to pass them on to her. This required *tremendous* effort. When I saw a bug in the house, I did not say "Ewww!" When my daughter started climbing trees and looked down at me from limbs above my head, I showed a brave face, masking my inner terror. It worked. My girls are now the first to pick up the worms, the spiders, or any other bug that comes into their path. They are old enough to know that mommy hates bugs, but they are past the stage when my tastes can impact theirs; their love of nature is already ingrained.

My husband would count his tendency to hold his feelings in among his weaknesses, so he makes an extra effort to express his emotions when we are with the kids. Like me, he wants our kids to learn the lessons he didn't as a child; he wants them to feel comfortable talking about their feelings. By being keenly aware of our own strengths and weaknesses, and by intentionally striving to overcome our deficiencies, we have been able to give them the best of ourselves.

16. Create a Family Culture

If you are partnered, set aside time together to decide what the family culture looks like and what the rules should be. This is a fun and exciting way to embark on the rest of your parenting journey as a real team and establish a foundation for you to return to. Once complete, involve kids in the Family Constitution, and update it regularly.

With a strong culture in place, kids gain confidence and pride in where they came from, becoming more connected with you. The tighter the familial bond, the greater their respect for you and the family, and the easier parenting becomes.

Once you establish your family culture, communicate it clearly to any sitters, nannies, or anyone else who watches your kids. Just as you would with a list of emergency contacts or a grocery list, pass along the Family Constitution. For example, if you want your kids to eat healthy, the sitter should not be breaking open her bag of potato chips in front of them.

Like every slice of your pie, this is a work in progress, but by being intentional in your parenting, you are going to proactively create the culture you desire and all of that up-front hard work will pay off in spades down the line. Intentional parenting will restore greater sanity, efficiency, and happiness to your home, making all of your slices easier—and what could be more delicious than that?

CHAPTER TEN

HEALTH

I'm so unfamiliar with the gym, I call it James.

— ELLEN DEGENERES

I know you don't need convincing as to the importance of this slice, but you might need to be talked into addressing it now. Though the strategies outlined below involve only minor modifications to your daily routines, they can have a profound impact on your entire life. Following them will give you a better chance of furthering all dimensions of your health, so that you'll have even more to put into the other six slices of your life. It pays to figure out where you are weak.

In chapter 1, I talked about the "I'll start when my youngest is in kindergarten" excuse used by countless women to delay their reentry to the workforce. Well, for the past few years, this is how I have talked about my nonexistent exercise: "When my son starts kindergarten I will have an extra hour a day and start working out." For years now, I have neglected my health, one of life's most important slices. As our lives get busier it is tempting, and at times even easy, to shove the health slice to the back burner or pretend it doesn't exist at all. We wait for an illness or a sudden weight gain or until we are huffing and puffing to keep up with our child to say, "Wow, I better make the health slice a higher priority."

I've got news for you: life does not favor those who delay. In the past four years, I went from being a fairly healthy person to one who suffers from consecutive illnesses. In one year, I was on four courses of antibiotics for persistent sinus infections. Last winter, I had a flu so debilitating that I couldn't leave the bed for five straight days over Christmas vacation. I could go on.

My history with health is a checkered one. As I shared with you, I was a competitive junior athlete, so exercise was not something I considered; it was built into my life in the form of daily multi-hour tennis practices and weekends spent at tennis tournaments where I averaged two matches a day. I had heard rumblings about my friends from high school using a StairMaster or eating frozen yogurt instead of ice cream to stay thin, but I didn't relate to that kind of thinking, as tennis kept me fit and healthy. As I shared with you already, once I got to college and eventually stopped playing tennis, I gained 30 pounds. I quickly discovered the impact that three giant bowls of sugary cereal every day could have on a body that had abruptly given up exercise.

Then there was the issue of my enormous boobs. Once I developed breasts at age 14, I suffered regularly from crippling stiff necks. On multiple occasions I had to default from tennis tournaments because I woke up unable to move my neck to one side. Big breasts ran in my family and having a triple D on my five foot two frame didn't just impact my neck, but also the kind of clothing I could wear. Shopping for a dress or a top or anything that hit the upper part of my body was severely painful for me; it involved tears, frustration, and ultimately compromise, not caring about design at all, only that my breasts were covered.

A year after graduating from college, I went to one plastic surgeon, who drew with ink on my breasts to show me where he would make the incisions and then sent me to a photographer's studio to have naked photos taken for the before and after. I still remember the studio and how cold and objectified I felt. In any event, I never got a second opinion (something I regret) and I went forward with the operation and the lengthy recovery, which included healing from the more than 1,000 stitches they placed across my chest.

Once I had a breast reduction, my neck and back pain disappeared, and I felt more active. Two years after I graduated from college, I got serious about my weight and health. I found my groove at the gym and cleaned up my diet, and I was completely amazed at how easy it was once I had lost the big boobs. I dropped the post-tennis poundage and felt fantastic for many years . . . until I got pregnant, at which point, I fell off the exercise wagon once again. That was 10 years ago. Since then, I have not exercised at all. Many times when women ask me how I seem to manage it all, I respond sheepishly, "I don't work out." I saw other women committing hours every week to their fitness regimen—hours I chose to dedicate to my career and my family—but coaching women gave me the kick in the butt I needed to get back to a regular exercise routine.

For so long, I had been ignoring my body. I am slender by nature and thus appeared healthy, but beneath the surface, I was a hot mess. Even though I knew quite well that a healthy life included a good diet, regular exercise, solid sleep, and stress management, my ugly truth was that I was stressed to the max, sleep deprived, and woefully out of shape. My diet was terrible, and I couldn't remember the last time I had sex with my husband. I was failing in each of these areas, and I couldn't accept this for myself any longer.

I pledged to myself that I would do better in all areas of health: sleep, eating, exercise, and stress reduction. I would go to bed by eleven each night, eat eggs for breakfast to get more protein into my carb-heavy and pescatarian—no meat but yes to fish—diet, find time for a walk three times a week, start reading a novel for a few minutes each night to relax my mind, and make intimacy more of a priority. The last of these meant getting into bed before I was dead tired and not allowing myself to use anxiety or exhaustion as an excuse for not taking the time to be intimate with my husband.

So many of us ignore our health, and we pay a heavy price. With our busy careers and family life, we don't carve out enough time to take care of our bodies, and over time we fall into ruts—or worse, our bodies succumb to more serious diseases that could have been prevented. I am not going to ask you to turn into a triathlete overnight or try to get you to become a vegan, but fortunately, there are a number of practical strategies that make self-care much more manageable in the context of your busy life.

Fill out this short quiz to see where most of your attention should go:

MY HEALTH NOW

Sleep _____
Sex _____
Fitness _____
Medical care _____
Nutrition _____
Relaxation _____

Score each category on a scale of 1 to 5, where 1 = "needs serious improvement" and 5 = "I'm doing awesome."

Now identify the two areas with the lowest scores and make those the first areas you tackle. For me, it was sleep and fitness that needed to change most dramatically. For you, it might be nutrition and relaxation. There is a lot of debate and discussion around which of these categories is most important, but for our purposes, we will weigh them equally. Take the test again every month and grade yourself on the past 30 days. The goal is slow improvement—when we make small, manageable changes and incorporate them into our lifestyles, they stick.

If you improve your scores in the health area, you will be a better partner, a better mother, and a better friend, worker, and contributor. You could be the hardest driver at the office but if you don't get enough sleep, you will not be as productive as you could be. If you don't relax and eat well, you won't have as much energy for your kids. For me, it has been adding weekly walks with friends and even one day a week with my husband, combined with the discipline to say no to *Homeland* if it is after 10:30, that has made a huge impact on how I feel.

Ingredient #1: Sleep

I used to be a nine-hours-a-night woman, but that fell apart fast when I became a mom. My oldest didn't sleep through the night until she was 14 months old. Afterward, back-to-back pregnancies and young kids made it so that unless I was traveling, I didn't get a night of uninterrupted sleep for seven years straight. I remember reading an article comparing lack of sleep with diminished mental capacity, and I believe it.

Sleep deprivation made me irritable and moody, and it also impacted my memory (those early years are a blur). Now that my kids sleep well, I do too and I am diligent about protecting my sleep by getting into bed by 10:30, turning off the phone and all devices, keeping the room dark, and making our bedroom a peaceful sanctuary.

When we sleep well and enough, we are better at work, better at home, and better to ourselves. According to sleep expert Dr. Michael Breus, a.k.a. "the Sleep Doctor," "Sleep is as critical as food, air, water, and shelter. Without it, all biological systems begin to deteriorate rapidly." Dr. Breus allows that genetics play a role in the need for sleep, but he notes that almost everyone needs at least 5.5 hours a night. Below that, Dr. Breus says, "we see significant detriments in function. I never endorse sleeping less than six hours."

Going to bed at the right time is also critical. Olympian Summer Sanders believes, "The more sleep you get in before the clock turns midnight, the more rested you feel no matter what time your alarm goes off." She calls sleep before 12:00 a.m. sleep doubled! Ever since she shared this principle with me, I have embraced it and know it to be true.

To help you determine more precisely when you should go to sleep, I suggest the following exercise that Dr. Breus shared with me. As he explained, the average sleep cycle is 90 minutes, and the average person runs through five cycles per night. That adds up to seven and a half hours of sleep. To determine your ideal bedtime, first figure out what time you need to wake up each morning and then subtract 7.5 hours. Spend two weeks going to sleep at this time—no cheating! If after two weeks you can wake up at your wake-up time without an alarm clock, you have found your ideal bedtime. If you still need the alarm, push your bedtime earlier. If you wake up an hour earlier than you needed to, you can go to bed an hour later.

In addition to figuring out your ideal bedtime, Dr. Breus recommends taking five basic steps to improve your sleep that you can start tonight:

1. *No sleeping in.* Stick to a consistent sleep schedule during the week *and* on the weekends, especially the wake-up time, no matter what time you go to bed.

2. *Stop the caffeine early.* Caffeine has a half-life of 8 to 10 hours. If you ingest caffeine after 2:00 p.m., you might have trouble falling asleep.

3. *Limit alcohol within three hours of your new scheduled bedtime.* It takes about one hour per drink for your body to metabolize alcohol, and the process can inhibit deep sleep.

4. *Don't exercise near bedtime.* The energy boost many people receive from exercise can make sleep more difficult. Stop exercising at least four hours before bedtime.

5. *Get enough sun.* Fifteen minutes of sunlight each morning when you wake up can help reset your circadian clock each day.

Ingredient #2: Sex

I am always amazed by how many women dismiss the need for a sex life. Some of these women wouldn't even dream of skipping a meal, missing out on precious sleep, or missing a workout, but somehow sex seems optional. Guess what? It isn't. A great sex life is good for your immune system, your blood pressure, and your heart. It reduces stress and pain, and by strengthening your pelvic muscles, it prevents incontinence in old age.[20] Sex also brings you and your partner closer, decreasing feelings of anxiety. Sold yet?

Sexologist Logan Levkoff advises that we aim for a "satisfying" sex life, but cautions that we each must create our own definition of satisfaction. Levkoff explains that your sex life "should be pleasurable and make you feel confident about yourself and comfortable in your own skin." Here are four tips she offers to bring about those results:

1. Look at your naked body and find three things that you really love about it. Your body tells the story of your life. Every mark or ripple is a badge of honor—if you learn to see it that way.

2. Fantasize about one thing that you have always wanted to try. If you are partnered, share this fantasy with him or her.

3. Aim for at least one orgasm per week, solo or partnered. Did I just say one? Try two!

4. Visit your gynecologist or another medical professional annually and talk about your sexual health. Are you feeling lessened desire? Pain? Are any of your medications impacting your sex life? Sexual function is a part of good health, and your doctors can help you to navigate your body better. When Mitch and I started going to bed earlier, our intimacy became more of a priority and I felt the benefits across all the slices of my pie.

Ingredient #3: Fitness

For many women, fitness remains a thing of their youth. "I used to work out a ton," Twitter executive Jennifer Prince told me, "but I have lost my schedule, my regular rhythm, and my drive to do so." Marketing director Nancy Blanchard in Boulder, Colorado, hasn't lost the drive to exercise, but much to her chagrin, she has lost her *ability* to make exercise happen. "I need to move my body more. Today I feel sluggish, but I remember the feeling of moving every day from my past. It's liberating and healthy, and I truly believe that it would positively influence every other aspect of my life."

Why don't you work out? Do you feel guilty taking time for yourself? A change in perspective can work wonders. One woman I coached told me that when weekends used to arrive, she dreamed of starting her mornings at the gym but felt too guilty leaving her kids to do it. I suggested that she think of exercise within the framework of her kids' lives. Working out meant that she was staying healthy, and the healthier she was, the longer she would be around to be their mom. On top of it, she would be modeling a healthy behavior for her kids. So rather than seeing her morning workout as taking her away from her kids, she could see it as significantly *enhancing* their lives, while also allowing her to feel great. This changed her outlook and she began working out on Saturday mornings while her husband was home with the children. Guilt-free.

Not all husbands are so supportive of women who want to exercise when it means they need to pitch in a little extra with the kids. In July 2015, I was interviewed for a *Wall Street Journal* article about how couples are competing for who gets to work out in the morning. It aptly called workout time the "land-grab of modern day parents." With the pressure to devote nonwork time to the family, working out can seem like a luxury, with tons of compromise involved from the one exercising and the one staying solo with the kids.

My advice is always the same here: you need to add working out to your calendar just as you would events such as a conference call or an important crosstown meeting. If your partner is more athletic or fitness addicted, he might claim that his needs in this department come first, but that's not the case. This is a vital activity for both of you. You both need workout time for the sake of good health, and those Sunday night planning sessions are the perfect time to navigate who is working out when. Add them to the family calendar just like you would your child's after-school swim class or a night out entertaining clients.

Besides relying on their partners, women I speak with devise all kinds of inventive solutions that allow them to weave exercise into their lives. For Jenn Feldman, owner of a Los Angeles–based interior design firm, the answer is bringing her exercise to work: "We started doing yoga together every Monday morning. It's a great way to set our minds and bodies for the week ahead." Debora Spar, president of Barnard College, observes that women who work out during the workday can cut corners to make it happen: "Work out during work hours if you can; hair can go unwashed if need be, and perfume does a pretty good job of masking sweat!"

Like many women, elementary school admissions director Nadine Zysman combines socializing with exercise time. She might make a date with a friend to hike, go on an evening power walk, or take a yoga class. "Exercise is more fun for me when I share it with someone I enjoy being with," she explains. Sales executive Felicia Alexander advises women: "Treat exercise like you would a meeting. By this, I mean schedule it so you have it in your calendar and invite someone to join you. Most mornings another working mom and I meet from six to seven o'clock.

It is wonderful for many reasons. If I didn't exercise in the morning I likely would not go at all, and I appreciate connecting with a friend before the start of my day."

If you can't find someone to watch your small children, there's an easy solution—take them! It was a meeting with a senior Wall Street executive that got nonprofit CEO Katie Hood moving again. The executive told her that her biggest regret at age 50 was not exercising when she was 40. So Katie, mom of four, now puts her two-year-old in a stroller to accompany her on her fitness walks. "I talk to her as we go. It makes the time go fast and it's quality one-on-one time we don't usually get." As kids get older, they can become exercise partners too, and the one-on-one time continues.

What if you simply don't have *any more* time in your day? You will be surprised to hear that you don't need it! Why? Done right, instituting a workout routine requires *zero extra time in your life*. As some of the women quoted above can attest, it has never been easier to integrate working out with your career obligations.

In today's office culture, executives and employees at all levels are encouraged to exercise, take walks, and swap the conference room for some fresh air. If you are in a job with a full lunch break, try eating your sandwich at your desk and then spending the rest of your lunch hour taking a brisk walk. We also live in a more casual world where your workout clothes and your work clothes might share the same section of your closet. When Tia went on a business trip to Charleston, South Carolina, she and her colleagues all agreed to pack hiking shoes and turn a half-day meeting into a hike. You can too!

And there is more great news here for busy women. If you choose moderate exercise like gardening or walking, the health benefits peak at four to six times per week. You can significantly lower your risk of heart disease, stroke, and blood clots. But if you opt for sweat-inducing, hard-core, heartbeat-thumping exercise, the benefits peak at just two to three times per week. So if you can, go hard! It really doesn't take much of a time commitment to get a seriously significant benefit.[21]

Ingredient #4: Medical Care

You never let your child miss her checkup. So why have you missed yours? Make regular checkup appointments and get to know your providers. As we discussed in chapter 7, your medical team is a critical part of your village. If you have a team of doctors you trust, you'll be ahead of the game when a need arises.

When Crayon Collection founder Sheila Michail Morovati's daughter cut her finger while cooking with her grandmother, Sheila texted her surgeon—whose number she already had in her phone—and he was able to assess whether her daughter needed stitches. That one text saved her an unnecessary trip to the ER. But how did Shelia happen to have her surgeon's number? As she explained, she works hard to develop close relationships with all of her health-care providers, and as a result, they willingly share their personal numbers or e-mails with her. I too have asked doctors for their e-mail addresses, and about half of the time they say yes. As with most things in life, if it's worth having, it's worth asking for! When you stay a step ahead—like having the doctors on speed dial *before* the emergency arises—you are better able to compartmentalize a crisis before it impacts all of your other slices.

Ingredient #5: Beauty

Maintaining your appearance may *seem* like a luxury, but it's a necessity. We feel more confident when we catch a glimpse of ourselves in the mirror and like what we see. If regular haircuts make you feel put together, incorporate them into your schedule. Kerry Faber, marketing director and mother of two, finds that she is "most successful when I make regular appointments for myself like my weekly pedicures in the summers."

North Jersey–based book publishing executive Kathleen Schmidt also refuses to skimp in this area; she believes that when you look your best, you feel your best. "I get a manicure and pedicure every two weeks," she says, "and highlights and a haircut every eight to ten weeks. My eyebrows get waxed every three weeks, and about once a month I'll schedule a facial. A woman who puts herself together well sends out a vibe of confidence."

I completely agree. Given my own unpredictable work demands, I need to have my nails groomed and hair blown out at all times; I never know when I might have to go on television on short notice. So instead of adding a new appointment each week into my already packed schedule, I plan my nail appointments, hair coloring, and blowouts well in advance. I consider these appointments part of my work. Regardless of your industry, you feel better when you take time to do the things that make you feel put together. Whether it is a facial mask or exfoliating regularly or taking the extra time to curl your hair in the morning, figure out what makes you feel your best and what is within your budget, and add it to your regular routine.

Right now, sit down and make a list of your "beauty nonnegotiables" and then schedule them in. If you need to color your hair every five weeks to keep the roots from showing, or if you need a professional facial once in a blue moon to manage clogged pores or fine lines, there's no reason not to book these appointments well in advance. When you do, keep the Golden Triangle in mind. All of these appointments should take place within the triangle between home, office, and your child's school.

Ingredient #6: Nutrition

The one element of good nutrition that I am just crazy about is water—I drink it constantly. If you can't count on your office environment for an endless supply of fresh water, bring your own. Nothing rejuvenates your mind and body like water sipped throughout the day.

But what about healthy food? Unfortunately, when we're rushing from place to place and feeding everyone else, our own diets can fall by the wayside. Nutritionist Keri Glassman believes it is never too late to start eating right. She shares the three big things you can do to change your diet today:

1. *Stay loyal to breakfast.* Choose two to three breakfasts that are healthy and that you love. Make sure to always have on hand the few items you need to whip them up fast. Breakfast is a can't-miss meal.

2. *Skip the unintentional sweets.* Unless it's a conscious indulgence, skip the sugar. This means no picking at birthday parties or bake sales, and no grabbing a Fruit Roll-Up because you forgot your own snack. What's a conscious indulgence? You eat a delicious, healthy dinner on Saturday night at a favorite restaurant and you have two or three bites of a blueberry crumble for dessert, passing the rest around the table.

3. *Go green at dinner.* If you make it your business to eat greens at every dinner, you are almost guaranteed to eat a healthier, fresher, more natural meal, aside from also packing in nutrients from the greens themselves!

I love these strategies because they are doable and achievable. They don't involve dieting or drastic measures; they involve small, easy changes to improve your health slice and incorporate a delicious, nutritious boost into your daily life.

Ingredient #7: Relaxation

It sounds so simple to say or think "Just chill," but we all know that what it entails is a whole lot more complicated. Neuroscientist Dr. Richard Davidson, one of the world's leading meditation experts, doesn't propose adding relaxation as yet another item to your already stretched day. Instead, he believes in sprinkling mindful moments throughout your daily life. Start modestly, enjoying mindful moments four or five times for two to three minutes over the course of your day. Do it when you have a few minutes to kill, like when you are waiting in line or sitting at a red light.

In the first chapter we talked about guilt as a predator and why you can't let it be yours. Guilt is wasted energy that steals our peace and our ability to relax, but fortunately, we can learn to control it. Once you take notice of times when guilt creeps into your thinking, you begin to have power over it and you can stop it from disrupting your life.

As Dr. Davidson explains, we can use mindfulness to help us ease any guilty feelings we may have. Using his mindful moment exercise, try releasing any guilt you feel each morning before you get into the car for your commute. Treat

---

DR. RICHARD DAVIDSON'S MINDFUL MOMENT EXERCISE

1. Use your breathing as an anchor. Don't change your breathing in any intentional way. Simply pay attention to the sensations in your abdomen or the tip of your nostril. Wherever you experience your breathing most prominently, use that as your anchor.

2. Once you can pay attention to five breaths in a row, allow the focus of awareness to expand to your entire body. Be aware of whatever sensations arise in your body—pleasant, unpleasant, or neutral—without intentionally trying to change anything.

3. Check in with your body. As your mind begins to wander, return focus on your body or your breathing.

---

this moment as an essential part of your morning routine, like stretching before a jog. Soon, it will become a daily habit, and one that allows you to be more effective and less encumbered. Create your own guilt-free mantra, or use one of these suggestions:

My work and my children and my relationships don't get the best versions of me when I feel guilty. Instead, I will be more present today. When I am at work, I will be fully engaged. The harder I work, the easier it will be to come home and give my full attention there. When I am at home, I will focus on my children and my partner. Just like my socks have a drawer, my energy needs to have its place. Being present allows me to be fully engaged wherever I am.

I am the best version of me because I lead a full life. I love, I work, I learn, and I grow every day. I am working for myself, for my family, and for the women who see me as a role model. Working gives me greater patience at home, and more decision-making power and more financial security for the entire family.

As we can all attest, when you return home to your kids after a long day, the transition can be tough. You're stressed out from work, and now you have to be there, really *be* there, physically, mentally, and emotionally, for your kids, who might have had a tough day themselves. Northern California–based psychiatrist Megan Lisska tried to manage this problem by having her sitter stay for an extra half hour after she arrived home from work so Megan could ease back in to her mom role. She soon realized that it wasn't working. Once her kids saw her at home, they only wanted her; the sitter's presence didn't help. So Megan developed a new system that has made all the difference: "I recognize the days when I need some wind-down time, and I go from work to a little café near my house. I'll sit there for 30 minutes, read something I want to read, answer e-mails from friends, catch up on social media, or maybe even just stare into space. Then I can come home recharged and, strangely, guilt-free."

Another way to reduce your stress load is to purposefully practice gratitude. This method works wonders for animation producer Koyalee Chanda. "We are not rich by any stretch. But just by virtue of having a home, toys, and clothes for the kids and an abundance of people who love us, we are privileged. I try not to ever take that for granted."

One family I know holds a gratitude session every night at the dinner table, where they go around the table and every child and adult shares one thing they are grateful for from that day. This is the kind of ritual that bonds a family and creates a culture of gratitude at the same time.

Body of Work

My own health program has changed since working on this book and yours will too. It didn't take much to feel better—I added three regular walks per week (hitting up the friends slice too!), began going to sleep by 10:30 as often as possible, and began booking regular checkups. By making even the smallest changes to your eating, your fitness regimen, your sex life, your medical care, your relaxation, and your sleep, you will find that your health slice is coasting. As women's wellness entrepreneur Tonya Lee Lewis says, "Think about your body as the multimillion dollar machine God gave you to walk through this life." When we see that perspective, it is hard not to want to add a little more sleep, exercise, sex, healthy eating, relaxation, and checkups to our lives. The more realistic the changes you make, the more likely they are to stick. If you maximize this slice, it will enrich your whole pie and give it a natural sweetener.

CHAPTER ELEVEN

RELATIONSHIP

The best thing to hold onto in life is each other.

— AUDREY HEPBURN

Your romantic relationship might not be unicorns and butterflies and bubble baths all the time or a helicopter flight to a remote island (though I highly recommend working toward that!), but it can still be a source of fulfillment, fun, and ultimately the connective tissue you need to keep thriving. This is the slice that often falls to the wayside and it is one of the last slices that you want to neglect. When your relationship is on solid ground, communication is better, your partner is more likely to help at home (which helps you have time for your career), and your kids benefit because when there is strength at the top, the whole family is rewarded. You are the epicenter of the family culture, and like parenting, you want to be intentional about the culture in your relationship. So, rather than thinking of this slice as the icing or, as it relates to sex and romance, as a guilty topping, let's acknowledge how critical this is for a healthy lifestyle and then let's talk about how we can make your relationship as successful as possible.

A Pie Life relationship has two main components: a productivity arm, which, as you'll recall, I refer to as the PartnerShift, and the romance, which I think of as the heart and soul of a relationship. Without both of these essential ingredients, your relationship slice can get stale or turn into a crumbling mess that falls apart on the plate. Either way, you want to do what it takes to keep this slice super flaky and delicious; after all, what fun is life if you aren't sharing it with a partner whom you adore? It is what will bring you joy and happiness for as long as you are on this earth.

But how do you do it? When you can barely make enough time to ask your partner how his day went or find the energy for an extended hug, how are you supposed to throw romance into the mix? In this chapter, we will focus on the highest impact steps that take the least time to do.

I used to say that the most important characteristic to look for in a potential partner was someone who thinks your quirks are cute. Now that I'm a mom, I think my top criterion has changed to finding someone who can tolerate your nuttiness. No work is harder than parenting. It can get under your skin and in every cell in your body—the exhaustion, the concern, the guilt. Yet it all becomes immensely easier when you have a loving partner by your side. Having someone at home on whom you can rely helps diminish the angst and exhaustion that "doing it all" moms commonly experience.

As wonderful as a supportive partner can be, of course, it's not a one-way street. You also have to put work into keeping your relationship rock solid despite the exhaustion you both feel and the hectic schedules you sustain. You and your partner are a team, and while it's normal for team members to argue and fight on occasion, you need to remind yourselves that you share the same goals and are working toward them each day, together. When you and your partner feel connected, it's easier to divide and conquer at home.

Relationships will wax and wane, as will the work you put into them. Amy Howe, COO of Ticketmaster and a mom of three, told me that she and her husband didn't do as much to nurture their marriage when their boys were "in the diaper years." Between the demands of parenthood and two busy careers, she felt there simply wasn't any time. But since Amy left her very busy job at a top consulting firm for her current position that requires far less travel, they have recommitted to spending solo time together. And they love it. "One of our favorite things to do is play paddle tennis together, followed by a relaxing meal over a nice bottle of wine. We are also incredibly helpful to each other during challenging times at work. Having your spouse as one of your greatest sounding boards and advocates is a privilege," says the 43-year-old.

Amy and her husband fell back into spending solo time together quite easily, but for some couples, a period of inattention can prove more damaging. When we become busy with kids and careers, it is easy to take our relationship for granted, but we cannot afford to let this slice go. Think of your relationship as the top of your family tree, because everything stems from there. When the couple at the top is happy and secure, the security and happiness fall down the tree and spread to the offspring. When we take time for our relationship, the entire home wins.

For a partnership to thrive, I believe you need five elements in place: a shared vision, weekly date nights (that's right, every week!), synchronized bedtimes, a daily check-in, and what I'll call "the little things."

A Shared Vision

To keep the connection intact even when you're being pulled in many directions, you want to maintain a shared vision of where you want your life to go—a combination of shorter-term and long-term goals that complete your view of your future. When you are each off spending your days in different locations and overwhelmed by a multitude of nonoverlapping concerns, you will continue to feel connected if you share a single big-picture vision for your life.

Whenever I have felt rudderless in my life, it was at times when I had no goals. And whenever I've felt stuck or stagnant in a romantic relationship, it has been because my partner's and my goals haven't been aligned. Nothing bonds a couple more than laying out goals and going for them. Would your team at work be successful without a shared vision? Of course not! Would the women's US soccer team have won the 2015 World Cup without a collective goal? No. You and your partner will feel infinitely more bonded with shared goals.

Before Mitch and I were engaged, we took a vacation to Lake Las Vegas. We spent our days there working out, eating a lot, and lying by the pool. Looking back now, those days seem like the world's greatest luxury. We felt no need to check our phones every few minutes to see if a child was in need, and we were completely free of guilt. It was just the two of us.

During that trip, we found ourselves spontaneously mapping out our vision for the future—and not in a type A, overly planned sort of way. Rather, it was more like a rolling, hazy dream.

"I would love to have many children," one of us said.

"Yes, three."

"Three! That's perfect. I want to live in a city where we can walk to get ice cream at night . . ."

"And I want to always make time for one another."

"I want to buy our first apartment by the time we have our first child."

We talked for hours, covering details big and small. At one point, Mitch took out a piece of scrap paper and scribbled them down.

We got engaged soon after that trip and were married six months after that, paying for the wedding ourselves (just as we had planned). We were pregnant two months later (even sooner than planned!). We bought an apartment, Mitch launched a company, we had another baby and then another, and I published four books. Ten years later, we were breathless, but we had achieved our collective goals, all while working as a team.

If you have not yet taken the time to map out goals with your partner, whether you've been together just a few years or a few decades, it's never too late to start. And I recommend starting big. It is easy to get into the nitty-gritty goals for next year, but it's more fun and engaging if you start with those "pie in the sky" visions. At times you will diverge or even conflict with your partner's dreams, and when this happens, it is time for a redreaming session. Spend two nights away together for an annual retreat to reassess your dreams and get you back on track. Or send the kids to your parents' or your close friend's place for the night and do it at home. Businesses do this to keep their employees connected and on track—why shouldn't you?!

Your vision will likely change over time, but the journey to reaching it will be your own personal bond that ties you together through the tough days and the great ones. One of the things that Mitch and I learned the hard way is how critical it is to celebrate little victories along the way.

Prioritize Date Nights

To maintain a close emotional and physical connection with your partner, regular dates are also essential. Think of them as your fuel; you need dates like a car needs gas. Twitter executive Jennifer Prince and her husband, Chris, like to meet for happy hour midweek to recharge and reset. Julie Wolfson, assistant professor of hematology-oncology at the University of Alabama, takes nightly walks on the way to dinner with her husband so they can talk without distractions. Investment professional Rosina Giuliante and her husband Chris, parents of a two-year-old, think of their Friday date nights as "our time to properly catch up on all the craziness that has occurred during the week."

Some couples opt to take their weekly dates during the day. Actress Susan Yeagley and her husband, Kevin Nealon, love to go to bed super early. "Date nights seem a little too ambitious and nerve-racking for us. So much pressure. We adore doing 'day dates' instead. This works out well for us because we have unusual schedules—some days working, some days not. While my son is at school, we can go out for a yogurt, go on a hike, or just pop popcorn at the house and watch old Alfred Hitchcock movies." She adds that she and her husband also find an occasional session with a couple's counselor to be "very therapeutic." Of course this day date schedule doesn't work for everyone, but the point is still worth considering—that you may need to think outside the box to make a date fit into your busy schedules.

If months have gone by since your last date night, bring it back—now! Put this book down and call a sitter! Make no mistake: sitting on the couch with your partner after the kids go to sleep is *not* a date. It is important to have that sort of daily time together, but if you're listening for a waking child with one ear, you're not fully present. Date night is about focusing on one another, and putting in a little effort to look good. Put on that lip gloss and let him change out of his grungy shirt. Date night is about sharing a fresh experience together in a relaxed environment. That can mean a drink at a local wine bar, a sunset stroll, or dinner and a movie—whatever works for you.

When you're out together, be sure not to use this precious time to complain or discuss the household or the next week's logistics. Don't talk about your kids' issues, that annoying comment your father-in-law made, or your challenging boss. Date night is not problem-solving time; it is time to enjoy each other. Talk about your hopes and dreams, share jokes, and enjoy each other's company like you did during those pre-kid days. Reacquaint yourself with the person you fell in love with in the first place.

A mom called my radio show to say that she and her husband had regular sex, but no romance. Their limited budget posed a problem; their children were small, and the couple had already tapped into her family for help with weekday child care. They couldn't ask their family for more, and they had no way to pay for a babysitter on top of movies or dinner. What should they do?

I suggested finding another set of parents with whom they could swap babysitting date nights. Until they found that kind of arrangement, they could create an in-home date night, with candles, a nice dinner and conversation, followed by snuggling on the couch with a movie. (Hopefully their kids would cooperate by staying in bed!) It's not the same as going out, but it's so much better than nothing.

No matter how exhausted you are (and I know that you are!), you can and you must make time for the regular date night. The payoff is enormous. Keeping the intimacy and emotional connection with your partner is essential—even more so in the exhausting early years. If you think you should go out only after you put your baby to sleep, think again. After going through the bedtime routine, you will never have energy for date night. It is one or the other and at the end of the day, no matter how tired you are, it is more tiring to do the bedtime routine than to go out to dinner. So tap into your network of babysitters or do a weekly babysitting swap with a nearby friend; give yourself at least that one night a week to go out and enjoy one another—and leave the baby talk behind!

Synchronized Bedtimes

Here's an easy solution to generating more intimacy: go to bed together! When your two warm bodies are in bed together night after night, sex will happen. Conversely, no matter how attracted you are to your spouse, if you are not going to bed at the same time each night, there is no way to rock the sex life. Seriously. You have kids, so a spontaneous midday or evening romp is probably off the table. That leaves you with nighttime sex, which won't happen if you are on your computer until one in the morning and he is snoring when you crawl into bed. I hear from so many couples that have fallen into this and practically live separate lives at night. It isn't just sex that gets lost when you only go to bed together one night a week. While you might not be swinging from the chandeliers while the kids are sleeping, it doesn't mean that there aren't benefits even beyond sex that make a synchronized bedtime worthwhile. There is cuddling and pillow talk and the intimacy that keeps the two of you connected. Conversely, when two partners are in two different rooms doing their own thing night after night, they turn into roommates. You do not want your partner to be a roommate. "Roommates" are headed for divorce.

Remember how much fun it was to go to sleep together early in your relationship? I promise, it's still fun. Mitch and I used to go to bed at different times, and we didn't share that closeness that I longed for. So now we aim to finish any remaining work by 9:30, which leaves time for an hour together most nights before a 10:30 bedtime. We can talk or do a puzzle or watch our favorite show (right now it's *Younger*) and be wowed together by all of the amazing plot twists, giving us one more experience to have in common. Snuggling up in bed like this will often lead to sex, a vital component of a healthy marriage.

Just because you are working hard and momming hard doesn't mean that sex should fall to the bottom of your list. Physical intimacy is essential for maintaining a bond with your partner. Dani Klein Modisett spent three years talking to happy, long-term couples for her book, *Take My Spouse, Please*. She concluded that, "Other than maintaining a sense of humor, staying connected physically is key in happy marriages. Get naked together. Don't let that piece go. If you lose that, you become very vulnerable as a couple." Unfortunately, relying on a once-a-week date night for sex is a poor strategy. You might not feel good on date night—you might be tired or bloated or stressed out. If this is your only opportunity for sex, then you're putting far too much pressure on it, and your sex life will likely shrivel up.

Should you schedule sex? Some people do, and like the at-home date, it's far better than nothing. "It sounds unromantic," *TODAY* producer Mary Ann Zoellner says, "but it is a necessity because if you don't, you can find yourself

---

ROMANCE FOR SINGLE PARENTS

If finding a new relationship is important to you, then date guilt-free and often. You won't find your next partner by dating randomly once every few months. When you are ready to meet a partner, make dating a priority with a weekly date night. Before you know it, you will be replacing the revolving door of dates with a person worthy of your weekly time and ultimately more. But the only way to find that new partner is to invest the time to meet and then cultivate the relationship.

Once you have a new romance in your life, then what? One of the most common questions I get from callers on my radio show is when to introduce a new romance to the kids. Simple: *only* introduce them to someone you can see yourself sharing your life with. Your kids do not need to meet flings or summer romances or the "in your life for right now" guys. If you are serious about a guy, you need to see how he interacts with your kids before taking a step like moving in together. When you first introduce your boyfriend, call him your "friend" and invite him to join you and your kids for a day at the zoo or a trip to the playground. Make it clear that he is not to touch you romantically during this outing. You are doing some important research here; you are observing his interactions with your kids. Is he making an effort to bond with them? Is it forced or natural? How are they responding to him? Does he appreciate your dedication to your kids, or is he jealous? Remember, you are not just looking for a partner for you, but a man who completes the family puzzle and can make it even stronger.

---

going months without sex." And even if you forego spontaneity, you can still weave in other surprises, like lingerie or a new location. One friend of mine meets her husband every Friday during lunch hour at a different hotel. As part of the deal, he has to show up with a new piece of lingerie each week. If this hotel/lingerie combination is a pipe dream and out of your budget, meet at home during lunch or lock the door to your office for a similar effect.

Remember, keeping the sexual spark alive isn't just about intercourse. It's also about little things, like holding hands or an impromptu kiss. Finance executive Andria Weil and her husband explain that, for them, "kisses involve holding one another, not just a peck on the cheek—and it makes a difference. We have a lock on the bedroom door and no TV in the bedroom." And that, my friends, is how they do it.

Bite-Sized Check-Ins

When it comes to maintaining a strong bond, staying in touch emotionally with your partner is every bit as vital as sex. If you can't share what's going on in your lives on a daily basis, you will start to share it with other people—parents, friends, and colleagues. You want your partner to be your best friend, and for that to happen, he has to be the first person you want to call when something good, bad, or funny happens. Communication breeds more communication. Take the childhood friend you haven't talked to in a year. Just *thinking* of calling her can feel exhausting because you have so much to catch up on. Yet the friend that you saw last Saturday feels more accessible. You can just pick up the phone and talk for a few minutes, since you don't have to fill her in on too many details.

Mitch and I do a daily check-in after our kids go to bed. We enjoy a glass of wine or a cup of tea together to unwind. It's a nice time to hang out and talk about our day, share stories, gripe about the overwhelming amount of homework our child came home with, describe any anxiety we're feeling about our work—whatever is on our minds.

One recent evening, I was relaying to Mitch my regret that I had double-booked us for holiday celebrations. I felt terrible having to tell the hosts about my error and awful that I had double-booked the kids. Since I had the chance to discuss this with Mitch face-to-face rather than merely texting him about it, he volunteered to stop working early that day so that he could take two of the kids and head to one holiday party, I could take our oldest to the other party, and we could all meet up afterward. Mitch is the one with whom I want to solve all my problems, big and small. It keeps us close, and we come through for one another in ways that continuously deepen our love.

You don't have to do check-ins the way we do; they come in all shapes. Florida-based couple Mandee Heller Adler, founder of International College Counselors, and her doctor husband, Jason Adler, make time at work to talk on the phone each day. This keeps them connected all week long in between their weekend date nights. Another woman I worked with named Kara has a day shift as an executive assistant and her husband, Remi, works the night shift at a factory. They check in in the morning after she gets the kids off to school and before she heads to work. She describes these daily 15 minutes as vital to their connection. Another couple I know checks in every morning while walking their dog together.

It helps to keep the check-in to 20 minutes or less so your partner will want to do it again the next day. Producer Mary Ann Zoellner takes the check-ins a step further by abandoning her TV watching completely in favor of talking to her husband. They don't just cover the kid stuff but also "politics, life events, and checking in with each other emotionally." Check-ins should be a true give-and-take; you both listen and share, lift one another out of bad moods, and give one another pep talks for the next day. They are about making each other the first responders—to be able to count on one another over our moms or friends or siblings. It is this daily interaction that keeps our relationship current and secure.

Staycations and Vacations

Nothing rejuvenates a relationship like time away without the kids. Mitch and I take one or two short trips a year, and we look forward to them weeks in advance. After we return, the memories we create keep us connected for weeks to come.

It was during the first overnight trip Mitch and I took together after relocating that we received the dreaded call. We had left our three young kids with their new nanny and traveled within driving distance but still a solid five hours away—far enough for us to completely focus on one another. One day into our three-day trip, we received a call from our daughter Ella's school; she had slipped and fallen. We spoke to Ella on the phone and then I called our pediatrician. He asked me to send him a photo of her banged-up head. I called the school nurse, asked her to take the photo, and once she did, I texted it to the pediatrician. He called me immediately and I will never forget the gift he gave me: "Whatever you do, don't come home. It is not a big deal. Give your nanny my phone number and if Ella feels badly tonight, I will personally go to your house to check on her, but do not leave your trip for this." In one phone call, he put me at ease about my daughter and took away all my guilt. This is where the whole "doctor team" concept we discussed in chapter 7 really paid off. Because I had invested in finding and building a relationship with our kids' medical provider, I could now spend time with my husband guilt-free.

It's so important to take regular time away to renew your relationship—and sometimes it's extremely hard. But do it anyway. If you've taken the time to build your village like we have, now is the time to use it. Former Olympian Summer Sanders told me about a man her husband, Erik, met who had been married for 60 years. How did his marriage last so long? He told Erik that he and his wife use the rule of sevens: a date every seven days, a night away without kids every seven weeks, and a trip without kids every seven months. "We have yet to really stick to it," Summer says, "but we think about it and we want to do it. One of these days . . ." What a great goal—an overnight every seven weeks! Even if you can't manage that ratio, make it a priority to get away at least once or twice a year.

These getaways don't have to be exhausting, expensive, action-packed adventures. They can be anything you want them to be. One of my favorite trips we've taken took place on our tenth anniversary. It was late January, and we went to a snow-covered, New England bed-and-breakfast. I had downloaded all 12 episodes of the true crime podcast *Serial*. Each night, we returned to our room after a delicious meal and lay in bed cuddling and listening to it. For us, this peaceful time alone was heaven. Interior designer Jenn Feldman and her husband swear by one-night staycations at local Los Angeles–area hotels. They arrive on Saturday afternoon, get massages, go to dinner, enjoy breakfast the next day, and return refreshed by noon on Sunday. Another option is to swap weekend babysitting with friends and do a staycation in your own home. Double sleepovers are fun for the kids too—everyone wins.

Psychiatrist and mom of two Megan Lisska told me that she was too obsessed with what she calls "the shadow life" to even conceive of a trip from her home in Northern California all the way to Paris. Megan defines the "shadow life" as the parallel life you must manage whenever you make plans: you plan your own time and then you simultaneously plan for the care of your kids during the same time frame. Megan's husband, Peter, insisted on the Paris trip, and in return, she insisted that he figure out the child care, not wanting the pressure of the vacation to weigh on her. Megan says, "Bless him, he pulled it off! We created a spreadsheet of child-care shifts, dividing them between our nanny and our favorite babysitter, with a few friends on call in case of emergency. It all worked beautifully, the kids were fine, and both nanny and babysitter would do it again." Not only did Megan have a great time; she learned that she had been too obsessed with the shadow life and felt grateful to her husband "for reminding me that most things are possible if you put your mind to them."

The Little Things

Another way to make sure the romance sticks around is to pay attention to the little things—to practice gratitude, buy a little gift, or just do a small favor for your partner. Research shows that successful couples have 20 positive interactions for every negative one. For Kerry Faber, Revlon's global marketing director, "the little things" means surprising her husband with his favorite chai latte. For another friend, it's writing little love notes on stickies and placing them in random places for her husband to find. Twitter executive Jennifer Prince tries to send "I love you" texts out of the blue, thanking her husband "for all that he does for me and our family." She also puts extra thought into the cards she gives him for birthdays and holidays. These small, seemingly insignificant actions are actually the bricks of your foundation, helping to keep you connected on a daily basis.

One great consideration when tending to the little things is to add in the element of surprise. Sure, it is important to acknowledge anniversaries and birthdays and holidays with cards and gifts, but it is also essential to do things when your partner is least expecting it. You can buy a card for him on the way home from work, bring home his favorite dessert to enjoy after the kids are asleep, buy tickets to an upcoming play or concert he loves, or, in the morning, give him a certificate to a massage to be cashed in that night. Keeping the romance alive is your job as much as his.

Invest Now

Your relationship with your partner is not one to put on the shelf for years to return back to once the kids no longer need your time. If we raise healthy children, they live with us for 18 years and then fly away to live their own independent lives.

Our marriages will outlast this time, and we will sail with our partner through the next phases of life together. That can only happen if we invest in our spouses.

Managing your relationship requires intention and care even during the exhausting labor-intensive years of parenting. Even when you aren't feeling it, give it. As Sherrie Rollins Westin of Sesame Workshop says, "If you want to be loved, be loving—even when you're often exhausted." If you water your relationship and feed it as one of your priorities over the years, it will bloom and keep growing. If you don't pay attention to it, it is not guaranteed to remain intact. So many women I work with laugh off their relationship and tell me they will spend time on it "later on," but it needs your attention now. We all get in ruts and we all get frustrated with our partners, but if you were once in love, you can fall back in love. When this slice is going well, the happiness and comfort you gain makes you more successful at work, a better friend, a healthier person, and a stronger parent. Love makes all of the slices go round!

CHAPTER TWELVE

COMMUNITY

Find a group of people who challenge and inspire you, spend a lot of time
with them, and it will change your life.

— AMY POEHLER

We talked earlier about creating a "village" for yourself, a personal net-work that functions as a logistical, emotional, and sanity-preserving support system. But a village is not enough. To live your life to the fullest, you also need to connect with a broader community of like-minded people. For most of us, a "community" is actually multiple groups, a Venn diagram of circles of people connected by our unique backgrounds and interests. Your community might contain people you know through your church, your book club, or your Wednesday night tennis group. Another woman's community might include people who participate in the school PTA, neighbors who live on the same block, fans of the local football team, and people who take the same dance class. Whatever community consists of for you, think of it as an added layer beyond your village, a physical place or a group of people you belong to that provides you with a strong, reassuring sense that you have like-minded people in your life, offering you a feeling of belonging. Without a slice of community, your pie is incomplete.

I like to envision community as a big net spread out below me in case I fall. Finding your community is vital to your emotional well-being and to your fam-ily's security. Like a trapeze artist, you need that broad safety net. A community supports the other slices of your life—your health benefits when you are part of multiple social groups, and your relationship benefits when you are not reliant only on your partner for companionship and shared interests. A community will not only add another dimension to your life, it will bring comfort and joy to your kids' lives as well. If you're reading this and thinking, "Oh no, I have no community," don't fret. It's never too late to create one.

When I look back at my relocation to Los Angeles, it wasn't just the village I created that made my new destination finally feel like home—it was the larger community I joined. This community was a combination of our religious circle, my children's school, my regular parenting group, and a collection of families that we meet with for dinner monthly. My husband's community was different. Initially, it included a group of dads he would see each morning when he walked Bowen to Starbucks to make the 5:30 a.m. wake-ups easier. Later, it included people he met while serving as a coach in AYSO (American Youth Soccer Organization) and running the annual Pancake Day at our daughters' school.

Our community in Los Angeles didn't just materialize when we decided to relocate there. We had to make it ourselves. When I flew cross-country to look at possible homes for our family to move to, I was with my oldest daughter, Ella, 5 years old at the time. I dragged Ella from house to house, hoping that our enthusiastic real estate broker and I could keep her entertained. I will never forget seeing a home that was likely way too small for our family of five, but on the day we visited, a smiling dad who lived on the other side of the street was teaching his 6-year-old daughter to ride a bike—midweek at three in the afternoon. And then I spotted two young kids playing basketball in the middle of the street on that same block. I was sold. We submitted the best bid our budget could allow. Sadly, we didn't get the house.

"Okay, no problem," I told my broker. "But that block is the only one I want to live on so please only show me houses there. Any house. But it has to be on that block." Our bewildered broker tried to talk me out of what she could only see as temporary insanity. Only 12 houses stood on that block, and just two of them had gone on the market during the previous four years. I explained that this block was the only one where I felt completely comfortable. In hindsight, what I couldn't fully articulate was that seeing the dad and his daughter with the bicycle and the boys playing basketball made me think that this block could offer us a community. And with three young children and no family or friends waiting for us across the country, that was what we needed.

As luck would have it, weeks later another home on that block came on the market. We made the first offer and got it. When we closed on the house, Mitch and I introduced ourselves to the neighbors. We met Kevin, the dad teaching his daughter to ride a bike, and his wife, Jen. When we asked what it was like to live in the neighborhood, Jen described the environment of my dreams, including parents standing outside enjoying a glass of wine together in the evening as the kids played. There was also talk of an annual Labor Day block party. It sounded heavenly. In reality, since we moved in four years ago, parents have gathered for wine only twice and Jen can't even remember describing this vision. But I still recall her saying it, and I remember the way it made me feel to hold the promise of a community in my hand. That promise was enough to subdue a lot of the fear I had about picking up and leaving New York.

All Shapes and Sizes

The more women I have spoken with, the more intrigued I have become by how vastly different, yet equally meaningful, women's communities can be. Don't limit yourself by thinking that a community has to look a certain way; it can take on a zillion different forms. They really do come in all shapes and sizes.

Angela Ferdig, a mother of two, describes her community as her former tennis peers, her kids' school (which is affiliated with her church), and people she has met through her career in the arts. Of these, church is especially important. She explains, "Our binding thread throughout the year is the church. Our school and church are one, making the school connections even stronger. Even though I'm not religious per se, there's something very comforting about seeing a family at a swim meet on Sunday morning and then seeing them again at mass on Sunday evening."

College advisor Mandee Heller Adler credits her religious community with making it easier to move to seven different cities over the last 20 years. Each time Mandee arrived in a new city, due to a job change or grad school, she reached out to the local synagogue to connect with others and to find her bearings. "I have always been welcomed with open arms, and I have found a shared kinship based on culture and background. This feeling of belonging has often provided the foundation of strength I have needed for other aspects of my life."

Another important source of community for many women is school. When Andria Weil first became involved with her children's school, it was to send her kids a message that she cared deeply about the people and institutions that took care of them. Andria has filled a variety of roles at school over the years, including board president, and the community has given back in spades. The support of the community has been felt, she says, "when pets and great-grandparents have died, when celebrating milestones, and in providing meals and visits when we've had illnesses, surgeries, and the rest. We are definitely not doing this alone!" As an unexpected and critical bonus, Andria found that her involvement has made it easier to help manage her children's dyslexia, anxiety, and ADHD issues. "Being involved in their schools and understanding how schools work has enabled me to be a more effective advocate for my kids," says Andria. While most parent activities take place during the school day when she is at work and unavailable, board meetings happen in the evenings, so she can weave them into her schedule. It might seem counterintuitive to add more commitments to Andria's already time-starved life, but her role as board member not only provided her fulfillment and a deeper connection to the school, but it enabled her to better manage her kids' circumstances as well. Precious time well spent. One big role is usually better than three small roles.

School has been an especially important source of community for my family as well. When Bowen finished his first year of preschool, a group of families from the school started doing a potluck dinner together every month. When one of the women in our group, Gelareh Gebayan, gave birth to her fourth baby, we all made meals for her family for the first week after returning home from the hospital. Gelareh, who's an emergency physician, tears up when talking about how much that gesture touched her. Even though members of this group did not start out as close friends, our monthly potlucks have now made us close enough to become vital members of one another's broader community.

Giving back is another great way to build your community. San Francisco–based Lisa Stone volunteers her time as an unpaid advisor to as many as four start-ups and nonprofits. Thanks to regular gatherings, the "brilliant women" who lead these start-ups have become part of Lisa's community. For Sherrie Rollins Westin, executive vice president of global impact and philanthropy at Sesame Workshop, community means being involved in activities where members of her family can help others. "When my daughter Lily was 15, one of the best things I did as a parent was to take her on a UNICEF mission trip to Brazil. We traveled deep in the Amazon rainforest to visit programs serving some of the most vulnerable children. I watched Lily go from being reserved and tentative to becoming a mini UNICEF ambassador, and I'm convinced it changed the way she looks at the world." The experience introduced both Sherrie and her daughter to a community of people who've bonded over a desire to serve others.

When I say communities come in all shapes and sizes I really mean it, because the members of your community don't even have to be human! "As a little girl," nonprofit executive Laura Dicterow explains, "my barn was my place of worship, my place to be present with the horses and mindful in a world that felt sad and unsafe for me." Over the years, the family that owns and operates the barn has helped Laura through her parents' divorce and later through her own painful separation. Her fellow riders are "a natural support system," taking care of one another's horses in times of need. But Laura relies most of all on her horse for comfort and support. "No matter where I am in my life, be it high or low, my horse is always waiting for me, nickering hello to greet me." Obviously the horse can't truly be her safety net by bringing her food or picking up her daughter when Laura needs to find her a ride last minute, but it is still a powerful example of finding ways to surround yourself with people (or, in this case, animals) in a place that gives you a strong sense of shared social values.

What if you didn't grow up with a strong sense of community? You might not be accustomed to bonding with people at school or through volunteer opportunities or even at your local barn. It doesn't matter—you can still become part of a community at any time. Author Dani Klein Modisett says she grew up with "zero community" so it took her longer to recognize the value it would bring to her life. But thanks to her religious faith, she became part of a community—slowly, gradually, without even realizing it. Dani, her husband, and their two kids have belonged to their Los Angeles temple for years. Over time, they have grown close to families who have children the same age as theirs; the parents have all known each other since the children were in preschool. Dani knows that she can count on this group if a crisis were ever to occur. "If I became ill, or dropped dead," she says, "this is a group that would absolutely show up for me and my family."

Build Community *Now*

Don't wait for a crisis. Start building a community well before you think you'll need it. Upon becoming a mom, Angela Ferdig found she wasn't quite connecting with other parents. They didn't seem to share the same focus, vision, or drive in raising their kids. She found herself missing other women who, like her, had participated in competitive sports, so she reconnected with her "sisterhood of tennis skirts" through Facebook. She recalls, "I suspected it was former athletes whom I needed to talk to, and I was right. I hardly knew many of these girls growing up, but today I have a deep connection with them. I think as children we were too competitive or too shy to connect, but now as adults and mothers we can put that all aside. For the most part, these bonds today are solely online, phone, or text. It mimics the schedule we had as kids when we only got to see each other at tournaments. But somehow these bonds are strong regardless of distance or time apart."

How strong? When Angela found herself divorcing with two young girls to take care of, it was her former tennis mates who provided her with the support system she needed. One woman from her college tennis team invited Angela and her daughters to visit her family in Bend, Oregon. Angela accepted the invitation even though she had never spent any time alone with this former teammate before. The two women hit it off in person, enjoying conversation, yoga classes, hikes, and cooking together.

On her last night of the trip, another tennis friend called. Upon hearing where Angela was, she said, "I'm jealous. Why did you go to Bend and not here?"

"You're next!" Angela said.

The trip and the friendly phone call that capped it off revived Angela and gave her a feeling of having "safe houses" throughout the world.

Angela sums up her community as "the Sisterhood of Traveling Pants . . . except I'm the pants, getting insight, support, and strength from all the strong women in my life whom I haven't seen in about 20 years."

Angela's experience suggests how helpful it can be to look to our past for sources of community, not just our present. When we leave a life stage behind, it can be hard to stay attached to the people we used to know. Make it a priority. Social media makes it so easy, and you can also do it the old-fashioned way by making an effort in person. Mitch and I bring our kids to three reunions every five years: his college reunion, my college reunion, and my business school reunion. Reunions are a natural and built-in way of staying connected with people with whom you will always have a strong shared allegiance. We always take our kids along when we can because it adds another dimension to these communities when our children feel a connection to the places and people that have played a prominent role in different parts of our lives. When we went to my last college reunion, we crashed with my friend Richy Lee's family in Milton, Massachusetts. His wife, Georgia, and their three kids welcomed us with open arms and we all got to spend the kind of time together that we never could have had if we relied only on the planned reunion activities.

The reunions you attend can be high school reunions, informal gatherings of former colleagues, or even meetings of military groups with which you served. My 81-year-old father still attends biennial reunions for his naval flight class. In the beginning, these occurred every five years, but as the men in his class got older, they changed it to every two years. As my dad explains, "It helps me relive a part of my life that I am very proud of. We were a very diverse band of brothers 60 years ago and we still think of ourselves that way. We make an effort to get together because, despite the fact that we are very different, we have this common bond."

Your community gives you a safety net, and it is critical to put energy into finding yours before you need it most. Don't wait for a crisis for humanity to rally around you. Having your community in place before you need to rely on it is the ultimate safety net for your family.

Your Community's Warm Embrace

What if you're not all that social, and you're intimidated by the thought of forming relatively loose, informal bonds with a wider group of people? My advice is to start small. Think about the groups you might like to join. If you have always wanted to be part of a softball team or a cooking club, now's the time. Go in with an open, friendly attitude and you will almost certainly be welcomed.

And if these sorts of groups don't exist where you live, why not start your own? When I arrived in California with my family, I realized that I didn't have many working mom friends around me. Rather than waiting for these moms to fall from the sky, my friend Leana Greene and I pulled together a handful of women to form a working-moms group.

Don't be hard on yourself if your first efforts at group building don't work. I tried to start a book club two years ago and failed miserably. One woman I invited declined to join, telling me that she already had a book club. I asked to join hers and she promised to "add me to the waiting list." I'm still waiting!

Keep trying, and over time, you'll build a community and enjoy its warm embrace. And hopefully you'll also experience the satisfaction that comes from *contributing* to your community. "Run to the fire," Wall Street maven Sallie Krawcheck told me when I asked her about the responsibility she felt to her community. "When a friend is in trouble—run, run." She continued: "This morning I e-mailed a woman who is in trouble at her company. Just a quick note to check in. Sure, you get another jewel in your crown in heaven but it also builds your community." Sallie understands what community is ultimately all about—giving as well as getting. When you feel that sense of belonging amongst various circles in your life, there is a confidence and a comfort and a safety net that comes with it. Putting effort into this slice impacts a multitude of other ones; it will help you make new friends, is good for your health, and is good for your family. What could be more satisfying and enriching than that?

CHAPTER THIRTEEN

FRIENDS

My friends are my estate.

— EMILY DICKINSON

Why did so many of us love *Sex and the City*? You've probably heard of food porn and real estate porn. Well, according to Kristal Bergfield, *Sex and the City* epitomized "time with friends porn." Think about it: we would sit and watch four women who were completely devoted to one another and their weekly get-togethers. When you were young, you could never have anticipated that a night out with friends would feel like a mini vacation in the middle of your week. It is ironic that as we get to the stage of life where we have less time for friends than ever, the importance of friendships in our lives is higher than ever.

Having a healthy slice of friends is essential for your health and happiness, and the benefits extend to your family. Recent studies have shown that our marriages are more likely to succeed if we have friends, that our kids are more likely to value friendships if they see us engaging in them, and that we will feel happier overall when we have more of them. And we're not just talking about nonrelatives here. Friends can include the sister-in-law you see all the time or the cousin who you adore. People who have a large network of close friends also enjoy better health and live longer, whereas close relationships with relatives or children have no effect on health.[22] And how's this for a powerful wake-up call about the importance of friends: a 2006 study of more than 2,800 breast cancer patients showed that those with 10 or more close friends were four times less likely to die from the disease than those without close friends.[23]

Why, then, do we allow ourselves to think of friends as an optional slice of our pie, or even a downright luxury? Many women I meet have trouble finding time for an active social life, and some neglect it entirely. They feel that it's too indulgent to even think of their friends slice when they don't feel they have enough time for their kids or their partner. As Oklahoma-based business development manager Catina D'Achille laments, "I am so wrapped up in work and my family that I rarely have girl time. I feel guilty for planning girl time when I'm already gone so much for work and traveling overnight monthly."

If you have been treating time with friends as a guilty pleasure, stop. Friends are a necessity, like eating right or getting enough sleep. During a dinner with girlfriends, my friend Amy Eldon Turteltaub shared her angst about leaving her 5-month-old daughter at home with her husband while she went to Africa to visit the set of a film being made about her late brother. Going on this trip would be a sentimental journey for Amy, connecting her with her childhood, and her presence on set was important to Amy's mom, Kathy Eldon. To alleviate her guilt, Amy was thinking of making the trip as short as possible; instead of taking a week or two, she would do it in just a few days. This would mean going all the way to Africa (a two-day journey each way) for just a couple of days on the ground. It was hard to see how such a short trip would allow her to spend real time on the set and connect meaningfully with her history.

Almost every friend at the dinner responded with a tale of leaving her own baby for a business or personal trip in the first year of their child's life: a week in London, two in Israel, two in India. They each had an experience to share with Amy. By the end of dinner, Amy was ready to book a more extended trip to Africa. She was doing it for herself, for her mom, and for her brother. And she left dinner a whole lot lighter. Though Amy and her husband enjoy a very close relationship, this outcome could not have come from a conversation with him. Amy needed the collective power of her girlfriends' experiences and perspectives to feel good about her decision and to take action.

That's just one example of how friends offer counsel about decisions big and small; they also offer us vital support, validation, and companionship when times are tough. In 2012, my friend Gila's mom, Mona Ackerman, died. Friends from all over the country flocked to New York to be by Gila's side. I will never forget looking around at her mom's funeral and seeing a collection of friends from each phase of her life: her camp friends, her childhood classmates, college friends, medical school friends, family friends, and friends from Boulder, Colorado, where she was then living. Gila had always been wonderful at making and keeping friends; her generous, kind, and positive spirit made her one of those people who everyone wanted to hold on to. Now, when she needed it most, all of those friends cast a web of support around her. She leads a very busy life but she always made time to keep up her friendships.

As we move through adulthood, we might feel that we don't need to make more friends—that our friend well is full. Not so fast! Nationally recognized friendship expert Shasta Nelson explains that the average person sheds half of their friends every seven years. This means you don't need to feel guilty about your holiday card list being a bit different than last year's. And friends fulfill different needs at different times of our lives. When we first get married, we tend to gravitate toward new couple friends for companionship. When we have kids, we need friends with children the same age as ours. When we become empty nesters, we need a whole new kind of companionship and other empty nesters to empathize with this dramatic life change. When we are widowed, we seek out other widows with whom to mourn and then rebuild our lives. Each phase requires additional friends. So no matter where you are in your life, it is always important to nurture your friendships—whether it's making new ones or renewing and strengthening old ones.

Persevere In Your Search for Friends

When I first moved to Los Angeles, I noticed a shocking trend. Nearly every woman I met talked about her "best friend." It became a running joke in my marriage. At some point during an evening with another couple, Mitch would kick me under the table at the precise moment when the woman's "best friend" was mentioned. Remember college and people gushing about their new boyfriend? It was just like that. We quickly decided that the best way to get adjusted to Los Angeles was for me to find my own best friend—fast. After all, Amy Poehler had her Tina Fey, Betsy Beers had her Shonda Rhimes, and I needed the Thelma to my Louise. It was my turn to find my BFF. (Though I couldn't believe that I was 43 years old and using that term!)

I played it much like I had the quest to find my husband: I hit the friendship dating scene hard. When I showed up for my first dinner with girlfriends in my new city, I wore a dress for the occasion. As I parked my car and approached the restaurant, my smile faded. My two new "friends" were watching me and whispering. My stomach sank; I suddenly felt like I was in middle school all over again.

"What's going on?" I asked, a question my eighth-grade self would have been too timid to express.

"We were wondering why you were so dressed up. We are in fleeces and you are in a dress."

"I dressed up for you," I said cheerily.

The rest of the dinner didn't go much better.

Then there was the time I arrived at lunch with Annie, an old friend from business school. Always one to have a story in my back pocket, I pulled out the "hilarious quest to find myself an LA best friend." I thought she would laugh with me but instead she explained why she couldn't be my best friend—she was taken. And before I could explain that this was my story *du jour*, not a legitimate quest for a best friend (or was it?), she interrupted my manic thoughts with this doozy: "I have the best idea. My husband, who you haven't met yet, really needs a best friend too. You would really hit it off. This is perfect. He will be your best friend." This wasn't the kind of BFF that I had in mind. Check please.

Months later, we went to the beach with another family. While our daughters splashed in the waves with their dads, Caroline (the other mom) and I stayed back in the sand with my youngest, Bowen. I shared that it was difficult for me to be turning a milestone age—40—after having just moved to Los Angeles 10 months earlier. I explained that while I had planned a party for my husband, who would be turning 40 a few months ahead of me, I couldn't do the same for myself because I didn't yet have a handle on who my friends were. "I totally understand," Caroline said. "The same thing happened to me when I first moved here. And then I met Lily. She completes my sentences. You will find a friend like that soon enough."

Back at home, Mitch commented that he had seen me "bonding" with Caroline on the beach. "I hoped you were opening up to her," he said. Did my husband really just say that? Had I entered a bad sitcom? "I did open up to her and she told me about Lily who completes her sentences," I explained. Another one bites the dust.

By this time, Mitch started feeling sorry for me. After yet another mediocre "first date," he said, "You know what? This is crazy. I can be your best friend. I *am* your best friend." Two days later, he recoiled: "I just spent a block walking behind two women who hadn't seen each other since the previous day. Just one day. But they had so much to say. Their breathlessness had nothing to do with their pace. It was a deep desire to share every minute of what had happened in their days. Their ability to share was beyond the capacity of what any man on earth could manage. I can't do that. You need girlfriends."

Of course I already knew that, but I had appreciated that Mitch had stepped up to the plate. I wasn't about to give up, because I had a trump card in my hand, and her name was Natalie Apple. Natalie had been my best friend when I had lived in Los Angeles 18 years earlier. Though we had lost touch and I had seen her only once (the first week we moved to LA), I felt better just knowing she lived there. In the back of my mind, I kept alive the notion that we would eventually fall back into "best friendom," just as we had been in our early twenties. Although she lived about 15 miles from me—that can be an hour drive in LA traffic—I believed that true friendship could overcome geography. Our shared history would prevail.

My hopes were dashed one day when I was in Harry's, the store where I bought all of my kids' shoes. As my daughters were taking turns in the shoe chair, I noticed a woman watching me. She approached confidently and said, "I know you from somewhere." We spent the next five minutes rehashing where we might have crossed paths. We went through colleges, neighborhoods, kids' schools, hometowns. There was nothing we could come up with. "Wait!" she exclaimed. "Are you Natalie Apple's friend?! She told me about you! Natalie is my best friend." I didn't hear another word she said after that; I was so intent on her not noticing the tears welling up in my eyes. I held it together in the shoe store and then slumped toward the car. "Did you hear that, Mitch? Natalie Apple has a best friend!"

He shot me a bewildered look. "But you haven't mentioned her in months."

"But I think about her!" I cried. He couldn't understand the significance. It was the final blow on the best friend mission. I was defeated.

You Don't Need A Best Friend—Just Close Friends

I didn't give up completely; I just changed my mission. Although I only infrequently had a "best" friend throughout my life, I always had a group of close girlfriends, women I'd held onto over the years from various stages of life. Each of these women meant a tremendous amount to me. Why, I now asked myself, should I suddenly transform into a "best friend woman" when what had worked for me in the past was having a small number of close friends?

I relaxed a bit and I started making some new "good friends." I had a friend from the Mommy and Me class that Bowen and I took together, a friend from Ella's new school, a friend from Ruby's school, and a new friend who, like me, had relocated. I even added Natalie Kiwi to the mix—she became a once-every-six-months "let's go for a hike" kind of friend instead of a best friend. After three years in Los Angeles, I could say, "I have many great friends. Not one, but many." I also tried to be better at picking up the phone and keeping in touch with old friends. I found that leaving a voice mail once in a while kept me connected. I also realized that the women I love seeing at my work conferences fill a friendship void, even if I only see them once or twice a year.

One of my favorite insights on deepening a friendship is this quote from Shasta Nelson: "Even if two people mutually like each other and want to be friends, they aren't friends until they develop a consistent pattern of positivity and revealing with each other." It's so true: if you really want to tighten your friendships, you must drop your facades and start sharing. I have taken this to heart by intentionally opening up to my friends, even if doing so puts me slightly out of my comfort zone. Like any relationship, you get what you give, and if you don't offer your vulnerable side, your friendship will never deepen.

Stay Open

Sometimes making a new friend requires a leap of faith. One day when we were on vacation in Utah, Mitch and I took the kids to Park City for the afternoon. Mitch left the store ahead of us and as he was walking down the street, a woman tapped him on the shoulder and asked, "Are you Samantha Ettus's husband? I recognize you from Facebook." Rachel Jensen Faucett was an old friend from my competitive tennis days. She was an excellent player from a big tennis family, but our contact with one another had been rather limited. The only time we had spent together was on the court as teenagers.

Rachel and I chatted, and we made plans to meet the next night for drinks and to catch up. It turned out that she homeschools her five children on a farm outside of Atlanta and is a well-known DIY blogger and Pinterest pro with almost two million followers. We were both working in the "mom" space, and she convinced me to be her roommate at a conference called Mom 2.0 Summit that would be held a few months later in Laguna Beach, California.

The conference was on the verge of selling out, so I knew that I needed to make a decision fast. I impulsively signed up to attend with Rachel and then e-mailed the summit cofounder, Laura Mayes, to say that I would be happy to fill in for any panelist that dropped out last minute. A week before the conference, Laura called with a spot for me, so I headed there with a speaking role and a new roommate in my old tennis friend.

Given our shared history, Rachel and I had a great time together. Since then, I have come to count her as one of my closest friends. She has come to visit my family in California, and we support each other professionally, sitting in the audience as cheerleaders for one another whenever our travel overlaps. I have spoken at the Mom 2.0 Summit three additional times since then and have met incredible women there. I am so grateful to Rachel for bringing it into my life.

When I share this story, people tend to marvel at a number of things. First, that Rachel was a person I never really knew. The time spent at drinks was the first time we had ever talked at length. Second, that we had drinks the next night after bumping into each other on the street after 20 years. We didn't just exchange niceties and make empty promises to keep in touch. Third, that when she proposed the conference, I went.

When faced with Rachel's offer, I could have immediately thought about all the reasons I shouldn't do it. Instead, I regarded Rachel's invitation as an opportunity to make a new friend, enjoy a new experience, and network for my business. It proved to be a win on all three fronts. And if it hadn't been? I would have lost a weekend. The next time you are faced with an unusual invitation or one that brings you out of your comfort zone, ask yourself if the potential reward outweighs the potential risk. Do your best to accept, even if you don't know exactly where the experience might lead. You might need to say yes to drinks with a new friend even if it means missing bedtime, and sometimes you might need to take the risk of asking another woman to lunch or dinner.

Find Friends at Work

People who have a best friend at the office are seven times more likely to be engaged in their jobs.[24] Just like you identified potential mom friends for your village, you want to identify potential work friends and make an effort to get to know them. If you are just intent on getting your job done and rushing to the six o'clock train, this can be a tall order. Our colleagues are often the last people we talk to (other than our roommates or families), and then we sign off for the day and don't see them again until the next morning. Not having a friend at work with whom to share a story from the night before, a tale from your commute, or the excitement of a new promotion can be lonely. You spend so much time at work and share a mission, so it makes sense that you might also share friendship.[25]

In looking for a work friend, it helps to find someone in a similar life phase and at a comparable level in the company, as your shared experiences will make it easier to develop a friendship fast. You might also want to target the colleague who seems trustworthy and low drama—you want your office friendship to be a source of energy and strength rather than negativity and gossip.

Look to Your Childhood

My friend Jason Levien has been part of my life since the tenth grade, when he dated a friend of mine. Jason and I were so close that when I broke up with my boyfriend the day before prom, Jason, then a freshman at Georgetown, drove to New York to sub in. Years later, he would name my first company, do free legal work for it, comfort me through breakups, and take walks with me when I carried infants in the BabyBjörn. We showed up for one another's weddings, birthday parties, and more. But what I most look to him for is his ability to be a "vault" for my life. He has a better memory for what has happened to me and what I've done or said than I do. We all need a friend like that. Including Jason, there are five friends from my early school years that I am lucky enough to consider "forever friends," and though we don't see each other often—sometimes missing years of one another's lives—I know that if I ever needed them, they would be there.

I'm not alone in valuing these oldest of friends. It was a childhood friend who helped Los Angeles–based media executive Felicia Alexander get "unstuck" after spending eight years in the same company. Felicia knew she needed a change, and this friend not only lent Felicia her resume template so she could update her own, she introduced Felicia to her own boss. That introduction led to a job offer that changed the course of Felicia's career. She spent the next two years learning a completely new industry, which she continues to enjoy and thrive in.

Childhood friends know our families of origin and the circumstances of our upbringing. Though you might be very different people today, the richness of that shared background is a bond that can last a lifetime, if you nurture it. It is never too late to rekindle that flame. If you haven't spoken to your best friend from high school in 20 years but you still think of her fondly, reach out to her. You never know where one olive branch will lead.

Maintaining Friendships During the Kid Years

During some life stages, friends take a backseat, most notably when you're parenting small children. Still, just as you want to maintain your career during this period, you also want to keep your friendships warm. And it doesn't have to take up a lot of your time. A Framingham Heart Study of more than 4,700 adults found that to have a great day, we need six hours of social time. If that sounds like a lot, the study defined "social time" broadly to include time spent interacting with colleagues or customers and corresponding with people over e-mail—basically any type of communication. If you add it all up, you might be a lot closer to that six hours than you think. And even if you're not, the study found that if you have at least three hours of social time a day, you reduce your chances of having a bad day to 10 percent.[26]

To stay connected with friends during your busiest years, you have to plan, and you have to get creative. On the planning front, "moms' nights out" are wonderful, and you don't need best friends to plan one. You can organize a moms' night out with other parents in your child's class or any other group you pull together. Every mom wants an outlet to spend time with other women friends and by being the organizer, you become part of the solution. Psychiatrist Megan Lisska of Mill Valley, California, notes that the most thoughtful gift she has received from her husband came one Christmas when he offered to spend a night at home solo with the kids each week so that she could do a weekly night out with friends. That gift made keeping friendships alive logistically possible and guilt-free at the same time.

When Danya Perry, chief of litigation for a finance company and mother of three, became single again, friends began to play an even more pivotal role for her. She works hard to fit them in and wills herself against feeling guilty about it because, she says, "Having friends and having fun makes me a happier person and therefore a better mother. That sounds like a rationalization, but it is a fact."

Friendship and _____ !

Your social life can easily be combined with other slices that are important to you, allowing you to save time while fulfilling two needs. Dr. Amy Wechsler, a dermatologist, encourages her friends to visit her in her office; they can have a quick skin treatment while they catch up for a few minutes. Not the right plan for everyone, including Stacey Bendet, the designer who founded Alice and Olivia. She learned long ago that this kind of arrangement doesn't work for her: friends and family would "stop by" and stay for three hours when she wanted to be working. So she now exclusively sees her friends out of the office.

Andria Weil combines health and friendship slices by exercising with friends. "I have one girlfriend who loves yoga so we will often meet early Sunday morning for yoga and a cup of coffee after." I too combine slices by getting my nails done every two weeks with Laurie Zink Haller. I get my beauty routine taken care of and stay connected with my close friend at the same time. And one of my favorite parts of traveling to conferences is that I get to further my career while spending time with friends, giving me an injection of social time while I am at work. *Marie Claire* editor in chief Anne Fulenwider also uses work travel to keep in touch with old friends. "One of the best things about business trips is being able to catch up with your old friend from high school who moved to Miami," she says.

Combining your friends and your children slices also works well. As I've mentioned, we always end our weekend by having another family over for a Sunday night playdate and dinner. PR firm owner Alison Brod does something similar: "Brunches and lunches with friends and your kids knocks it all out, and everyone has fun."

And then there are "girls' weekends," which can be great for your health and your friendships. The concentrated time is unparalleled in terms of keeping you connected in a way that catching up over a meal cannot. But the women I have met who have had the most success in this arena are the ones who are religious about planning these weekends far in advance and being committed to making them happen. Megan Lisska has two regular weekends on her annual calendar—one with her high school girlfriends and one with her San Francisco–based book club. What do they do on these weekends? Megan shares: "There is always a spa and lots of wine involved, and lots of talking, talking, talking late into the night. I guess it's the grown-up version of a slumber party." This can be challenging logistically and you might be feeing guilty leaving the kids, but when you strengthen your friendships and take a break from your regular routine, you will return healthier and happier, and this makes you a better parent.

Keeping in Touch

Still think you have no time for friends? Cherell Harris, an associate director of bulk technology based in Wake Forest, North Carolina, feels like she should spend her limited free time with her husband and two sons since she works and attends law school at night. Yet Cherell compensates by using her commute to call friends. Even when you can't reach your friend, a voice mail can be enough to keep the friendship alive. My dear childhood friend Lara Sass and I met in the eighth grade. We have not lived in the same city in years but we still stay connected. There have been stretches where we don't reach one another for six months at a time, yet we manage to stay connected through voice mails and texts. Those are enough to say, "I'm thinking of you. You are on my mind. I may not see you often but I still feel close to you and always will."

When my life gets super busy, I press "like" on my friends' Facebook photos for five minutes or send a "thinking of you" text. These are quick ways to keep a friendship alive without a ton of output. Florida-based ad sales account executive and mom of three Ashley Sanchez and her friends rarely get together, but they use social media to keep in touch. My college roommate Laura detests small talk, so she keeps in touch by sending me links to articles or sharing her son's favorite books, knowing that he and my daughter have similar tastes. I'm not saying that's the same as deeply sharing, but a little can go a long way in terms of keeping these friendships active and warm.

The Clutch List

You might not be able to *always* be around for your friends, but all of the women I interviewed talked about showing up for friends when they needed it most. Sometimes I like to play a game with myself, thinking about whom I would call if I really needed help or comfort. Do a little tally for yourself of who you can count on in a clutch and turn the tables on yourself too—who can count on you in a clutch? It helps to think about these close friends in your life and how you can maintain your bond with them.

Shasta Nelson recommends having a few friends to rely on so that when you need one, you always have one there. She explains that when you find yourself being resentful of one friend for not being "there" for you, you should take it as a sign that you need a couple more.

Good Morning America contributor Tory Johnson considers her husband, Peter, to be her best friend, but she also has three very close girlfriends: "The people I jokingly refer to as my 'bail list.' We'd drop anything for each other." When I was in New York recently, I saw my dear friend and business school classmate Michaela Clary. We hadn't seen one another or even talked for the past nine months, but when I saw her we picked right up where we had left off, and the time in between never made me feel less close to her.

Friends serve different purposes in your life. However you incorporate them, they are worth the effort—your health and your happiness depend on them. You can whip up the greatest, most delicious pie in the world, but if there aren't enough friends in the mix, your pie will still be only half-baked.

CHAPTER FOURTEEN

HOBBIES

If you are losing your leisure, look out! It may be you are losing your soul.

— Virginia Woolf

When my grandmother, Miriam Waldman (a.k.a. Mickey), moved into assisted living in 2001, she had to give away boxes of her beloved Harlequin romance novels. We all laughed when we tried unsuccessfully to donate them to her local library; they were deemed too lowbrow. But these novels had meant so much to my grandmother, and her appetite for them was insatiable. She would devour three a night!

She had recently lost the love of her life, my grandpa, Avery Waldman, the man with a giant personality who had not left her side since she turned 15. As trashy as the Harlequin books were, they filled the gaping hole left by my grandfather's death. They were not her only comforts, of course. She had her weekly card game and her favorite television shows and the pleasure she took chatting with family and friends around her kitchen table over her beloved store-bought pastries. Only when her eyes went and she could no longer read a book or even focus on her favorite TV show did she pass away. In other words, until the day she died, my grandma didn't lose sight of her hobbies slice of her pie—nor should you. The "hobbies" slice is the easiest one to abandon, especially when you lead a hectic life, but it's one absolutely worth fighting for. When you are busy with your other slices and time is scarce, your interests can seem discretionary, but they can also be a major source of happiness, a critical driver of productivity, and an awesome opportunity to connect with your children. The research backs this up! And hobbies have staying power; like friends, it is never too late to pick up a new one or return to an old one.

Productivity Enhancers

Hobbies don't just offer enjoyment throughout our lives; they keep our minds sharp and make us more productive. Hobbies enhance your performance at work and at home.[27] They also boost brainpower as you age.[28] Researchers from San Francisco State University studied 350 people across a variety of industries and with varied hobbies, and they found that those with a hobby outside of work scored 15 to 30 percent higher on performance rankings than those without a hobby. The hobbyists were also more apt to help their colleagues.[29]

Hobbies like gardening and crafting ease stress, improve happiness, and protect the brain from aging.[30] Google acknowledged this impact when it launched a "20% time" rule, allowing employees to spend 20 percent of their time doing passion projects. Smart companies have long recognized that people are more productive when they take breaks to tinker and experiment with their own ideas.

When we pursue our passions, we grow and engage a part of ourselves that otherwise lies dormant. This can open up new career possibilities for us and expose us to pockets of interesting new people and cultures.

Make Time for Hobbies—With Your Kids

When we hear the word "hobbies," we tend to think of activities like collecting rare coins, or hiking or needlepointing. Let's expand your definition to include *anything* that interests you and that you make time for. It could be exploring new cuisines or learning piano or a new language or salsa dancing.

Single mom Rita Meyerson is a full-time consultant in New York and is getting her doctorate in Washington, DC, yet she still practices her favorite hobby, yoga, three to four times a week. She explains, "I have done this by remaining laser-beam focused on my priorities—mom, career, and my well-being—and I eliminate any distractions that get in the way." Laura Fairchild Streicher and her husband met in Malibu while surfing. Although her life is now far busier, she still surfs. If she can make time for her hobby with two kids and a two-hour daily commute, so can you!

And find ways to include your kids. This is how they learn to find and cultivate their own passions and interests. For Kimberly Van Der Beek and her husband, James, travel is a way to include the whole family in something they love. They hop in the car with their three kids for road trips and they consider the journey to be the destination.

Kerry Huggins Svrcek, mom of two in Cypress, Texas, works full-time in the insurance industry and counts real estate as her hobby. She involves her kids by bringing them along to weekend open houses. Fashion executive Melissa Klostermann has chosen soccer, hiking, skateboarding, and tennis as her main activities because her 9-year-old daughter likes these sports, and the two can enjoy them together. To *Hamptons* magazine editor in chief Samantha Yanks, "Hobbies mean family time," so Samantha, her husband, and their daughter all play tennis together. Boston-based consultant Jessica Stokes is passionate about gardening. While she works in her garden, her 6- and 10-year-old kids play in the yard or read on the porch. If they want to help, she pays them— a penny a weed.

Tory Johnson and her daughter Emma have always enjoyed crafting together. As Tory describes it, they would get a creative bug once a month, each time exploring a new craft: from decoupage plates to iron-on patches and jewelry making. The two would buy every supply imaginable at Michael's craft store, watch YouTube videos on technique, and do it over and over again until they got it right. It was this hobby that eventually turned into a business for Emma, who launched Em John Jewelry while in high school and has already achieved so much success that she has paid for her first year of college.

When I was a young girl, I too loved to make jewelry. Many people around me thought that tennis was my hobby, but I thought of competitive athletics as more like my job. Making jewelry, however, was my favorite activity. My mom and I would make trips to the bead store in downtown Manhattan and I would spend hours selecting beads. When we returned home, I would turn the beads into necklaces, which I then sold. I loved going into stores and asking the clerks to take my creations on consignment, or sitting with a friend in Central Park and selling my necklaces on top of a cardboard box in front of the tennis courts.

I have passed on this passion for beading to my daughter Ruby. In Ruby's last year of preschool, I brought her to a bead store with an area in back where customers could sit and create jewelry. She not only enjoyed our time there but she felt terrific when her teachers proudly wore her necklaces and gushed over her creations. Ever since, at the end of every school year, Ruby uses her keen eye to make beautiful necklaces for her teachers as thank-you gifts.

Reconnect With Your Past

Many women I meet manage to stay connected with lifelong passions they developed during their own childhoods. These not only bring up fond memories but also help them weave together the stories of their lives. As busy as they get managing jobs and children, they still find some time to squeeze them in. Dani Klein Modisett has long counted dancing as the key to her happiness. No matter how crazy her life gets as an author, wife, mom of two, and caretaker of her elderly mother, she gets to a dance class at least once a week.

Erin Alberte of Elms Grove, Wisconsin, has three kids and a demanding job as a recruiter, yet she still makes time to race sailboats on an all-women racing team, a carryover passion from her youth. She does it by leaving work early and making sure her husband puts the kids to bed solo on those nights. After Erin races, she enjoys dinner and beer with her crew and makes it home before ten o'clock.

As a store manager and mom of two teens, Gretchen Kelley of Duluth, Minnesota, works just as hard to incorporate her long-time passion for running into her busy life. She runs early in the morning and sometimes in the evening, and when she brings her daughter to soccer games, she often puts in four miles while her daughter's team warms up. She explains that other parents probably think she's crazy, but she knows she is a better parent when she takes the time for herself.

I never miss an opportunity to stay in touch with my childhood love of crafts. One summer, my 4-year-old son Bowen and I discovered beautiful orange and yellow jingle shells on a beach in Shelter Island, New York. We returned repeatedly to the same beach all summer long to collect them. Then we went to Kmart and bought glass jars. We carefully cleaned the shells (a nice lesson in assembly line operations for Bowen, who liked to be part of the quality control team!), dried them, and added them carefully to the jars. These displays became the perfect décor for our living room shelves, and we both feel a sense of pride at our very tangible accomplishments.

The Pleasures of Play

When you don't make time for play, you and your loved ones pay the price. As New York–based psychotherapist Juliet Keeler-LeBien cautions, "When we do not have outlets, we can feel frustration and resentment, since all we are doing is for other people. Without nurturing our creative and curious needs, we can feel isolated, exhausted, and depressed." Though this slice tends to be universally smaller than most of the others, it adds essential flavor to your life. Without your interests, life becomes bland. With them, life gets sweeter.

Once you decide on your hobbies, try to come up with creative ways to make time for them. In the early years of parenthood, your time will be more limited or sporadic but as your kids age, you will have more room for this slice of your pie. Whether knitting on the sidelines between your child's tennis matches or antiquing on a Sunday with a child in tow, if you decide hobbies are important to you, you will find a way to do them. Hobbies are like old blankets and a warm cup of soup, always there to return to in sickness and in health, in

HOW TO FIND A HOBBY

1. *Think back to childhood.* Did you enjoy softball or the violin or collecting stamps as a child? Maybe it's time to start a new collection or pick up that old sport, instrument, or pastime.

2. *Look at a course catalog.* Go to your local college, pick up the evening class schedule, and skim through it. You will be amazed by how many of the classes spark your interest. Whether it is watercolor painting or introductory animation, website design or creative writing, take one.

3. *Tap into others.* Ask friends, Facebook peeps, colleagues, clients, and neighbors about their hobbies. Not only is it a great conversation starter, you'll uncover a treasure trove of enticing ideas.

4. *Get reading.* Expand your horizons by delving into websites that cover everything from crafting to sports. Notice what attracts your attention.

5. *Dive in.* Trying a new hobby is risk-free, so take a class or start doing it and only then determine your passion for moving forward. If you don't click with the new hobby, move on. There is an endless well from which to choose.

happy times and rough ones. They're consistent, they often don't require much money to keep up, and they're comforting.

We know that play is essential for children's brain development and for them to become healthy adults, but what about the impact of play on adult health? In an NPR piece entitled "Why Adults Need Recess Too," various experts explain how playing is not only how we connect, but it also keeps us sharp.[31]

Virginia Woolf was right: if you lose your leisure, you really do risk losing your soul. So let's transition from ignoring your hobbies to seeing them as a slice that you intentionally prioritize. One way to do it guilt-free is to include friends or make an effort to make new friends who share your hobby. Like having friends, having hobbies makes you healthier and more well rounded and fulfilled. You might miss a bedtime to meet your running group for a sunset run in the park, but there are six other nights in the week and this could be your partner's special night with the kids. Busting out the violin does not have to feel like a guilty pleasure. Your interests are an essential part of who you are; if you want to honor all of yourself and nourish yourself, you need your hobbies. Take out the paintbrush or the soccer cleats and light the flame. Keeping your interests alive is a vital part of achieving a rich and satisfying lifestyle.

CONCLUSION

I choose to make the rest of my life the best of my life.

— LOUISE HAY

I was nearing the end of this book when my own pie began to crumble. It started with a strange tingling in my back that my doctor told me was likely a pinched nerve. A few days later, I was in the midst of the back-to-school frenzy with my kids when I found out that the numbness and intense pain I was feeling were the symptoms of shingles, a painful and debilitating rash that lingers for months.

That same week my beloved father was diagnosed with bladder cancer, and a few days into the second week of school my daughter caught pneumonia, which kept her home for more than a week, and then our nanny quit. Around that time I received an e-mail out of the blue from a woman writing a book about a monster from my childhood. The author wanted to interview me about my old tennis coach, who had turned out to be a pedophile (discovered after a dramatic, high-profile, failed abduction of the student he coached after me). The nightmare from my past that I had successfully buried for more than 20 years was coming to surface whether I liked it or not. And oh yeah, there was this looming book deadline.

But there was also my daughter's eighth birthday party and a Break-the-Fast we host for 100 people every year for the Jewish holidays. And I received some incredible news that my first book—published more than 11 years earlier—was being republished by Barnes and Noble and I was asked to revise the introduction. Life wasn't going to stand still for illness or the return of a childhood nightmare.

The lesson? Life is messy and unstoppable.

We all know that the best pies are gooey and sloppy and never look exactly as we conceived them. Just like our lives, our pies are delicious as they ooze their imperfections. Every day is a series of moments both good and bad. Tom Hanks once described his love for wife Rita Wilson this way: "Life is one damn thing after another. It's much more pleasant to go home to someone you like." His description of life made me laugh. Life *is* a series of moments, and it helps to not only surround yourself with people you like, but also to expect that tough moments will come along with the wonderful ones. It will be choppy and messy and smooth and rich and crunchy and delicious—sometimes all in one day. If we expect smooth sailing, life is endlessly disappointing. If we can laugh through the bumps while expecting things to more often go right than wrong, we can really seize it.

When Andria Weil, Boston-based mom of three, and her husband finally were off to a weeklong skiing vacation with their kids, they decided to bring along their young au pair so they could steal some couples time during the trip. They also had to incorporate work into the mix, so the au pair would be a valuable extra set of hands when Andria was working on Monday and Tuesday and her husband was working on Wednesday and Thursday. They intended to have some quality time with their kids, time for each other, and time for work. So that the au pair could have some fun too, they signed her up for ski lessons.

That Monday, their vacation fell apart when the au pair broke her femur on the bunny slopes. As Andria describes it: "In one afternoon we went from having child care to having another, injured child to take care of."

Suzy Welch still remembers the feeling of running home late from her job as editor in chief of *Harvard Business Review* on a night when too much was going on at the office for her to be anywhere but there. The then single mom walked in to find her four kids patiently sitting at the dining room table, food untouched, waiting for her to eat with them. Five minutes into dinner, Suzy heard her phone ringing and dumped her bag on the table to locate it in a frantic haze. She took the call and found out that she had to turn around and head straight back to the office. The episode still haunts her. As she describes it: "That was in 2001, and it still makes me want to weep. Incidentally, I've asked, and not one of the kids remembers that incident. But I will never forget it." These kinds of stories are important for us to hear and share with one another because no matter what our profession or circumstances, we all experience the same problems, and no matter how much we try to control every piece of our lives, it will be messy and imperfect.

When I had shingles and my dad was sick and I was under intense work pressure and everything felt overwhelming and unpredictable, I still went through my life as usual because I had no choice but to do so. I still played my roles of mom and wife and writer and radio host and friend and community member and daughter and sister and board member and all of the other titles I hold. Yet if you follow me on social media, you wouldn't have heard about my illness or my dad's condition or any of the other calamities that felt like invasions into my daily life. Why? Because although I live my life out loud in many ways, when things get serious, I get private. Not so private that I don't tell friends or family what is going on, but broadcasting my ills on Facebook would be my version of complaining about car payments at the office water cooler. Some places are better for rosy talk. Social media is one of them.

When I interviewed designer Stacey Bendet, she told me how funny it was when people were "amazed" that she worked up until the day she had her baby. She described how the distraction of working and momming and daily life helped her, that if she had stayed home to focus on every ache and pain, she would have felt worse. So for me, I chose not to tell my book editor that I was dealing with all of this.

When I shot the photo for the cover of this book, I couldn't feel my left side. I remember the photographer touching my left shoulder to move it to a more flattering position for the picture and thinking, "Holy cow. I can't feel my left side." But once I finished the shoot, I was so happy I hadn't said anything. Had I mentioned the shingles, my editor might have suggested postponing the shoot; or felt guilty giving me tough edits to handle, and I really wanted to keep things on track. I wanted to feel normal at least for a few hours during my day even when most things didn't feel too good. Over time, my shingles healed, my dad was on a speedy road to recovery, and life returned to a less frenetic and crisis-filled pace.

Though our pie slices are interconnected, it is critical to see them individually when we lie in bed at night ruminating about our day. When you think about your pie, you must avoid the temptation to consider only the slices that aren't going well. To do so is the equivalent of cheating on the pie—it is like taking bites of the pie without asking. The beauty of the pie method is that you must contemplate each of your six or seven slices every time you start wallowing in one or two crummy ones. When you do this, you can't help but be grateful for what *is* going right and fixing the struggling slices becomes a whole lot easier.

Now that you have joined me on the journey of the Pie Life, I hope you feel inspired to take bites out of life that you never dreamed possible—to partake in the whole pie rather than just focusing on three or four slices. A full pie incorporates all of your slices, and you are deserving of the most complete and delicious pie possible.

Devour it!

ACKNOWLEDGMENTS

It is said that the only ones who like to hear thank-yous are those being thanked but, as a reader, I often find myself skipping directly to the acknowledgments before I delve into a book. I learn volumes about the author from those pages, a window through which to see some of the characters who make up the mosaic of an author's life. As this book is a personal one, I suspect you will know me fairly well before you make your way back here.

About a month after this book was complete, my mom passed away suddenly following a swift five-week start-to-finish battle with lung cancer. In many ways, this book only exists because of my mom. As my brother so eloquently wrote in her obituary, "She will be remembered by those who knew her well as a fiercely loyal advocate and an equally spirited adversary." My mom had a forty-seven-year love affair with my dad, and together, they modeled what an equal relationship and an equal place in the world looks like.

There are so many people who supported me as I initially muddled my way and eventually soared through this process. I am so grateful to Rebecca Raphael, who not only introduced me to Ghost Mountain Books, but was also the first reader of the book; she makes my writing pithier and funnier than I ever could. My gratitude goes also to visionary Lisa Clark, who believed in this book from the start; to the ever positive and efficient Carly Stratton; and to the savvy and talented marketing force Andrea McKinnon. Thanks so much to Heather Adams and her team at Choice, with whom I clicked from the very start. I am always in awe of Jennifer Joel, my agent for all five of my books. Thanks also to my amazing TV manager Cameron Kadison.

A huge thank you goes to my brother Tim, who is not only my dear friend, but also my harshest critic and best editor; he reworked hundreds of columns for me years ago when I had a syndicated weekly column with Scripps Howard and has remained a sometimes reluctant, but always pivotal, part of my writing process. When Tim told me that *The Pie Life* was excellent, it was akin to a blessing from the Pope. Thanks also to his wife Courtney, who is not only family, but a cherished friend and source of moral support.

I have always had an insatiable appetite for women's stories and in the case of *The Pie Life,* there were more than one-hundred women who shared theirs candidly with me. I interviewed them and, in some cases, badgered them for ultrapersonal details of their lives. Thank you to Morra Aarons-Mele, Erin Alberte, Felicia Alexander, Stacey Bendet, Kristal Bergfield, Nancy Blanchard, Alison Brod, Ramy Sharp, Koyalee Chanda, Jane Condon, Michele Costa, Laura Dicterow, Catina D'Achille, Kerry Faber, Jenn Feldman, Angela Ferdig, Jennie Finch, Sara Fisher, Laura Flynn, Kelly Flynn, Anne Fulenwider, Rosina Giuliante, Erica Hagen, Leslie Hale, Cherell Harris, Mandee Heller Adler, Katie Hood, Amy Howe, Tory Johnson, LaNae Kelley, Gayle King, Dani Klein Modisett, Melissa Klostermann, Emme Kozloff, Sallie Krawcheck, Alexandra Lebenthal, Megan Lisska, Samantha McGarry, Eleanor McManus, Heather Mellish, Rita Meyerson, Sheila Morovati, Heather Norby, Danya Perry, Jennifer Prince, Audrey Puente, Sahara Pynes, Autumn Reeser, Gregg Renfrew, Shonda Rhimes, Summer Sanders, Kathleen Schmidt, Maria Seidman, Laura Slabin, Debora Spar, Jessica Stokes, Lisa Stone, Sally Susman, Ashley Svabek, Marisa Thalberg, Kimberley van der Beek, Amy Wechsler, Andria Weil, Suzy Welch, Sherrie Westin, Deb Whitman, Julie Wolfson, Emily Woodward, Janet Wright, Samantha Yanks, Kalika Yap, Tanya Yarbrough, Susan Yeagley, Shelley Zalis, Mary Ann Zoellner, Nadine Zysman, and a host of other women who did not want their names revealed. They were all so generous in sharing their stories and giving us a glimpse into their worlds. Some of their stories ended up on the cutting room floor, but that had absolutely nothing to do with their value and everything to do with the editing process.

Thanks to some of my readers and editors, Seth Schulman, Amy Slothower, Jason Levien, Kelly Taylor, Jon Ford and Jonathan Peck. And to my childhood and college cheerleaders who have been by my side at every turn. Thanks also to my many newer Los Angeles friends who already feel like family; I am indebted to them for their care of me and my children.

And thank you to my entire extended family: my Aunts Rozie and Linda, and especially my dad, who gives the best advice and who, along with my mom, has held an unwavering belief in me throughout my life.

For my daughters Ella and Ruby and my son Bowen, for whom my love knows no bounds: Thank you for being my most loving supporters and for keeping me in check by quoting me back to myself.

And finally, to my husband, Mitch. Thank you for supporting my dreams, for pushing me to do better, for loving me flaws and all, and for partnering with me in living The Pie Life.

NOTES

1. http://www.amanet.org/training/articles/Time-Outs-Take-an-Increasing-Toll-on -Womens-Careers.aspx

2. http://hbswk.hbs.edu/item/kids-benefit-from-having-a-working-mom

3. https://www.propublica.org/article/false-rape-accusations-an-unbelievable-story

4. http://www.nytimes.com/2015/07/19/style/marlene-sanders-a-force-in-tv-journalism.html _r=0

5. http://www.webmd.com/balance/features/is-guilt-getting-best-of-you

6. http://www.nytimes.com/2015/01/04/magazine/the-complicated-origins-of-having-it -all.html?_r=0

7. http://observer.com/2015/09/uncharted-territory-a-mother-of-three-navigates-the -world-of-the-newly-single/

8. http://psychcentral.com/lib/the-paradox-of-pushing-kids-to-succeed

9. http://www.statisticbrain.com/new-years-resolution-statistics

10. https://www.psychologytoday.com/blog/dont-delay/200806/goal -progress-and-happiness

11. https://hbr.org/2014/12/rethink-what-you-know-about-high -achieving-women

12. ibid.

13. http://www.usnews.com/news/articles/2012/06/22/vive-la-difference-gender -divides -remain-in-housework-child-care

14. http://www.theatlantic.com/sexes/archive/2013/06/the-distinct-positive -impact-of -a -good-dad/276874/

15. http://www.smithsonianmag.com/ist/?next=/smart-news/daughters-who-see-their-dad -doing-chores-have-less -stereotypically-female-career-aspirations-180951609/

16. http://nymag.com/thecut/2015/08/why-we-need-older-women-in-the-workplace.html?mid =fb-share-thecut

17. http://www.reuters.com/article/us-usa-commute-costs-idUSKBN0E721M20140527

18. http://time.com/3709816/moderate-exercise-is-best/

19. http://www.npr.org/sections/health-shots/2014/05/26/314602190/anxious -parents-can-learn -how-to-reduce-anxiety-in-their-kids

20. http://www.webmd.com/sex-relationships/guide/sex-and-health?page=3

21. http://time.com/3709816/moderate-exercise-is-best/

22. http://www.webmd.com/balance/features/good-friends-are-good-for-you

23. http://jco.ascopubs.org/content/24/7/1105.full

24. http://psychcentral.com/lib/the-importance-of-friendship

25. https://hbr.org/2013/07/we-all-need-friends-at-work

26. http://www.gallup.com/businessjournal/127043/friends-social-wellbeing.aspx

27. http://www.nytimes.com/2007/12/02/jobs/02career.html?_r=0

28. http://www.nydailynews.com/life-style/health/hobbies-boost-brainpower-age-study-article-1.1476227

29. http://www.npr.org/sections/health-shots/2014/04/17/303769531/could-those-weekend-pottery-classes-help-you-get-promoted-at-work

30. http://www.cnn.com/2014/03/25/health/brain-crafting-benefits/

31. http://www.npr.org/sections/ed/2014/08/06/336360521/play-doesnt-end-with-childhood-why-adults-need-recess-too